OUT OF THE

ORDINARY

STONEWALL INN EDITIONS
Keith Kahla, General Editor

OUT OF THE ORDINARY

ESSAYS ON GROWING UP WITH

GAY, LESBIAN, AND

TRANSGENDER PARENTS

NOELLE HOWEY AND

ELLEN SAMUELS, EDITORS

ST. MARTIN'S PRESS ✹ NEW YORK

"My Mother and the Nun" by Kelley Conway
originally appeared in *Girlfriends Magazine*,
November 1998.

"Sexual Healing" by Noelle Howey originally
appeared in *Ms.*, October/November 1999.

"Moral Fabrics" by Jennifer DiMarco originally
appeared in *Generation Q*, 1996.

All other pieces © 2000 by the individual authors

www.stmartins.com

Book design by Victoria Kuskowski

Library of Congress Cataloging-in-Publication Data

Out of the ordinary : essays on growing up with gay,
lesbian, and transgender parents / Noelle Howey and
Ellen Samuels, editors.
    p. cm.
    Includes bibliographical references.
    ISBN 0-312-24489-4
       1. Children of gay parents—United States.
    2. Gay fathers—United States—family
relationships. 3. Lesbian mothers—United States—
Family relationships. 4. Bisexual parents—
United States—Family relationships. I. Howey,
Noelle. II. Samuels, Ellen Jean.
    HQ777.8.O87 2000
    306.874—dc21   00-025493

First Edition: August 2000

10 9 8 7 6 5 4 3 2 1

To our parents, Dinah Howey-Mouat, Christine Howey,

Stephen Samuels, and in memory of Myra Samuels,

with affection and gratitude

CONTENTS

ACKNOWLEDGMENTS

We wish to give thanks to a number of individuals who offered their time, enthusiasm, and expertise, and who helped us get the word out: Jordan Samuels; Meema Spadola; Sarah Saffian; Abigail Garner; Ophira Edut; Kerry O'Quinn; Brian Gossh; Elizabeth Wales; Gilda Bruckman of New Words Bookstore in Cambridge, Massachusetts; Stefan Lynch; Hannah Doress; Emily Bender; Rebecca Edelson; Felicia Park-Rogers and the wonderful people at COLAGE; Drs. Leonard and JoAnne Podis; Joy Goldsmith; Booh Edvardo; Jamison Green; Kathryn and Elie Herzog; Ilene Sperling; the Cambridge Lavender Alliance; and Peggy Gillespie, among others.

Thanks to our incisive editors at St. Martin's Press, Abigail Rose, Kristen Macnamara, Teresa Theophano, and Keith Kahla. For wonderful support at every juncture, we are truly grateful to our agent, Karen Gerwin, of ICM.

Much love to Meagan Rosser and Christopher Healy, who not only contributed insightful essays but also provided unwavering support and insight. Finally, we are indebted to all our writers for their courage to tell the truth.

PREFACE

Dan Savage

Shortly after his first birthday my son figured out how to turn on the TV set. D.J. wasn't walking yet, but one day, as my boyfriend and I watched in horror, D.J. crawled to the table with the TV on it, pulled himself to a standing position, and pushed the button that brings Elmo into our house. Then he plopped down on the floor, quickly slipping into a vegetative state.

"Our work here is done," I said to my slack-jawed boyfriend. "All he needs now is a Marilyn Manson CD and some violent video games and he can pretty much raise himself."

When my boyfriend and I decided to adopt, a lot of our older gay and lesbian friends were horrified. Having kids, one over-sixty gay male friend told me, was the primary thing the gay and lesbian liberation movement liberated him from. For many gay men his age, kids were an unhappy accident, part of a sinister plot hatched by the heterosexual conspiracy to keep them closeted. Kids were the spring in the trap: A closeted gay man would date women in order to fool his parents, employer, and God, and in order to fool the women he was dating he would go through the motions. He may have planned a short period of opposite-sex dating or even marriage—one or two years, tops—which he could then point to for the rest of his closeted life as "proof" that he was straight.

But then he'd go through the motions one night and a condom would break, or a diaphram would slip, and Mr. Closet Case was suddenly Mr. *Married* Closet Case with Kids. Extracting yourself from a relationship involving children, as many straight people can tell you, is infinitely more complicated than extracting yourself from a childless relationship, so many closeted men and women who had kids felt they were doomed to the heterosexual lifestyle for the rest of their lives. Since it wasn't until very recently that out gays and lesbians could have children—heck, it wasn't until very recently that gays and lesbians could be out at all—a fair number of the adult children of gays and lesbians kicking around today were conceived in early, ill-advised heterosexual relationships that fell apart. Their queer moms and dads toughed it out for as long as they could before they could no longer deny who they were, and made coming out a game the whole family could play.

The stories of today's adult children of gays and lesbians are compelling, but fortunately, the more negative circumstances of their young lives—the closet their parents conceived them in and subsequently emerged from—are gradually passing away. By the time my son and his generation of kids raised by gays and lesbians—kids whose parents were never closeted—are old enough to share their stories, having queer parents won't be as remarkable as it is today, and with luck, their stories won't be as painful or harrowing.

At least I hope not. In a review of *The Kid*, the book I wrote about the difficulties we faced adopting D.J., Stephen McCauley wrote in *Newsday* that "as for the special difficulties faced by the children themselves, we'll have to wait for D.J. to write [his] own memoirs." Just in case people twenty years from now are still curious enough about the experiences of the children of gay men and lesbians—curious enough to buy a book like this— we're not going to let the TV, Marilyn Manson, and video games raise our son for us. We're going to have to be good parents, just in case.

FOREWORD

Colonel Margarethe Cammermeyer, Ret., Ph.D.
With her son, Tom Hawken

MARGARETHE

When I finally acknowledged my lesbianism to my four sons, I had been divorced from their father for nearly ten years and was all but forced to come out to them. My sexual orientation was about to become public knowledge. After twenty-seven years of service, I had challenged the military's antigay policy and the press was going to write about it.

As a parent I agonized over how to be appropriately truthful with my sons, who ranged in age from twelve to nineteen. Would my children want anything to do with me if they knew? The fear of rejection—of being disowned and discarded—was overwhelming.

Telling them was as hard in some ways as I had anticipated. After I told them, "I am a lesbian, and the army is going to discharge me," my youngest son, Tom, looked away—as I'd feared he might—and did not want to talk about it further. But they had a few surprises in store for me as well. My eldest said, "Oh, mother, we've known for years." My sons made it clear that they supported me wholeheartedly in my challenge of the military's antigay policy. They felt that, after my loyalty to the service, the discharge was unfair and senseless.

My sons had figured it out long before my disclosure to them. But in my self-absorption at the time, I had not fully understood the ways in which my new identity as a lesbian mother would impact my sons. Just as I had to make decisions about who needed to know, my sons, too, had to determine what to say to their friends. Because my military case became so high profile, they were forced to deal with the fear of taunts, like "Your mom's a queer, a lesbo—you must be one, too." My boys feared possible rejection from their friends just as I had feared losing my family and friends.

Besides fear of the narrow views held by much of the outside world, my sons also had to deal with their own stereotypes of homosexuality. In addition to overcoming the fundamentalist religious view that being gay is "against God," they also had to confront the issue of the "gay lifestyle" and determine whether it was *my* lifestyle. As I heard their discussions of how they disapproved of the so-called gay life but accepted me and my partner, Diane, I was at first taken aback and then angry. After all, I thought, gay people exist in every aspect of society. They earn a living for themselves and their families, serve in the military, pay taxes, belong to a spiritual community, and participate in making America a better place. What lifestyle does that constitute, exactly? I believed when people talked about "lifestyle," they really meant sexual conduct. And what adults did in the privacy of their own home was no one's business.

My sons had always been accepting of me. The difficulty had been the explicit news of my sexual orientation as a lesbian. What my sons eventually realized was how insignificant my sexual orientation was in the content of my relationship with them. Moreover, they saw the love that Diane and I had for one another. Even Tom, who had some qualms in the beginning, became a proud advocate.

In 1998, Tom took a hiatus from college to work on my campaign for Congress. He said, "When issues of family values come up in the campaign, I want people to see me standing by you." I asked him how he was so sure of himself and of me. He said he had been raised to know and love me. Nothing had changed, he said, just because people knew I was gay.

TOM

When I was younger, before my mom came out, my brothers and I always knew that there was something different about her. We had a hunch that she was a lesbian, but we never talked about it. No one else did either, although my father would occasionally make a snide comment—a comment we would all try very hard not to register.

I can remember exactly when my mom told us the truth. My brothers, Mom, and I were in the car on a back-country road. She was picking us up after one of our visitation days with Dad. She pretty much just said, "Hey guys, I'm a lesbian," and our response to that was an equally casual, "Yeah, tell us something that we don't know." In some ways, I think that we were already fairly at ease with the idea of her being a lesbian before she even told us.

Going through grade school there didn't seem to be any problems. When I entered high school, though, it was a little harder: My peers were definitely filled in on the facts about my mom. Few ever said anything, but I could tell at the time that they looked at me differently. I told myself they were uneducated high schoolers, and comforted myself with a circle of great friends who stood by me every inch of the way. In fact, that was one of the very best things about my mom's coming out: I found out who my friends were.

In the last few years, learning that my mom is a lesbian has opened my eyes to the diversity out there in the world. It's helped to teach me that everyone should have the opportunity to be happy without others passing blanket moral judgments. Above all, it's reminded me how much I love my mother and that I couldn't be prouder to be her son.

MARGARETHE

Coming out has been an extraordinary journey for me and for my sons. After years of hiding, this process has taught me what it feels like to live honestly and openly. Still, I know that every day I have to decide how I will come out to someone. If I hold a magazine with gay content, should I roll it up to hide the cover? If people ask me about my "husband," should I correct them and talk about my life partner? My children and grandchildren must continually decide when and to whom to divulge that Grandmother is a lesbian who is in a long-term, committed relationship with a woman.

My sons and their wives, my grandchildren, and their buddies are a part of Diane's and my everyday life. We are truly blessed with their acceptance and love; we are blessed that they recognize all of our similarities, not our differences.

As the lives and stories of nontraditional families are portrayed on television, and in movies and books, all our lives will become easier. We will learn to use different words to ask questions about families. One day we will be able to enjoy the uniqueness of our families without fear of rejection. It is important to remember that accepting and embracing same-sex couples and their families does not diminish the institution of heterosexual marriage or those families. Rather, it illustrates the diversity of our common humanity, which is to be valued and treasured.

INTRODUCTION

Noelle Howey & Ellen Samuels, editors

When Noelle was seventeen years old, her government class launched into a discussion of whether gay parents should be allowed to adopt. While she sat quietly, uncomfortably pretending to doodle in her notebook, the honor students around her shouted out such vitriol as, "A dyke could never raise a normal kid" and "Gross! A gay guy would probably molest his son if he had one." The teacher nodded, acknowledging every view—even the most hateful ones—as equally valid. When Noelle finally nervously ventured the possibility that the child of a gay or transgender parent might be well adjusted or even straight, she was ridiculed by her entire class, who collectively declared such a thing impossible. Noelle tried not to cry for the rest of the period. After all, her father had just come out as transgendered.

For years, people have talked *about* the children of gay, lesbian, and transgender parents. Pundits have weighed in on whether it's just too hard on the kids to be in a family that doesn't conform to the Mom-Dad-Kids-Dog model. Activists have battled in the legislature and the court of public opinion over custody and adoption rights for gay parents. Gay people themselves have spoken about how parenthood jibes (or doesn't) with gay culture, what it's like to fight for the right to love a child, and whether gay parents are intrinsically different from straight parents. But few people—whether psychologists, politicians, or other so-called experts—have listened to those who were raised by gay and lesbian parents, to hear the stories of what it's like to grow up in a family that society deems atypical, or even abhorrent. No literary vehicle had allowed these writers to speak for themselves rather than report on how they feel through interviews or research studies.

We discovered this silence almost by accident. In 1998,

while Ellen was working at a feminist bookstore in Cambridge, Massachusetts, she was struck by the number of customers who asked if there was a book for teens with lesbian parents to read. Ellen did some research and found that nearly all books for children of gay parents were aimed at the elementary school set (i.e. the infamous *Heather Has Two Mommies*). There was little material of sufficient emotional depth that might speak to an adult audience. Although Ellen does not have gay parents herself, as a lesbian, she found this absence disturbing.

Meanwhile, Noelle had just been equally struck by the tremendous response she had received for an essay about her transgender father published in *Jane* magazine. Significantly, the essay generated a number of anguished letters from other children of transgender parents—people who had felt quite alone until finally reading about an experience much like their own. Once the two of us began talking about these events, we quickly realized there was a definite need for a book such as this one, and we began seeking out contributors—a process that proved to be lengthier and more complex than either of us anticipated.

Unlike the many media networks that connect gay, lesbian, bisexual, and transgender people, there are very few organizations or media that connect their children. We found our talented pool of contributors through a combination of word of mouth, Internet postings, flyers at conferences, and diligent research. Many of our contributors are accomplished writers; others are novices, with whom we worked closely to evoke the full power of their stories. We are excited by the geographic and class diversity among our contributors, yet we also acknowledge that we were unable to achieve as diverse a group as we would ideally seek out. Although our contributors represent a range of racial and ethnic identities, we would have preferred to find more contributors of color to give even greater balance to the collection.

That said, *Out of the Ordinary* collects, for the first time, personal essays by the children of lesbian, gay, and transgender parents.* These essays range in tone from humorous to poignant, fearful to accepting, and angry to hopeful—sometimes all at once. We hear from professional writers and from college students; from radical activists and from conservative Christians; and from straight, gay, and bisexual children of gay parents. These essays explore the thorny, painful, and often funny experience of growing up with a gay, lesbian, or transgender parent in a world where lesbianism may be chic on the cover of *Newsweek*, but not necessarily in the girls' locker room. For instance, Laurie Cicotello, a conservative Republican, explores what it was like to have her father come out as transgendered yet remain loyal (and married) to her mother. Peter Snow delineates how his lesbian mother continues to live with her husband despite carrying on a love affair with a woman for five years. After living through fifteen years of abuse from his straight, alcoholic mother, Jeffrey Wright explains how a kindly older gay man became his adoptive father. These are only a few examples of the many compelling stories we have collected.

During the eighteen months we spent compiling the essays for this book, we heard certain common refrains from contributors, the most frequent being, "I wish I had had a book like this when I was a kid." Of course, young people of today are growing up in a very different world from that of twenty, ten, or even five years ago. Today, they can see characters with lesbian mothers on TV shows like *Beverly Hills, 90210* and *Popular*, join organizations like COLAGE (Children of Lesbians and Gays Everywhere), or use the Internet to find information, support groups, and chat rooms for children of gay parents.

Despite how far we've come toward cultural acceptance and visibility of so-called "alternative families," it is nevertheless clear that parents and children today still face intolerance, which can range from name-calling on the playground to legal persecution and denial of custody. Currently, the vast majority of states do not allow same-sex adoption, and custody is routinely denied to gay and transgender parents. Since same-sex marriage has approached legalization in several states, the backlash against gay families has taken the form of federal and state statutes that specifically define marriage as only between a man and a woman. This definition not only invalidates same-sex partnerships but suggests that the growing number of single-parent families are also somehow inferior to the traditional heterosexual nuclear family.

In the course of working on this book, we came to realize just how much progress still needs to be made before the gay movement will achieve parity for its adherents. For example, we initially sought to have all our contributors proudly named and even photographed with their parents. We soon realized that that would not be feasible, as we lost dozens of potential writers whose parents were still closeted. Finally, we relented (six of our contributors have written essays under pseudonyms) in the hope of showing how a life lived in secrecy affects—and often infects—a family. We also, sadly, came to realize that a number of our contributors are either estranged from or angry with their gay parents—but not for the reasons the punditocracy might think. These writers are not upset that their parents don't sleep with members of the opposite sex. They aren't resentful that they have been deprived of a "normal" upbringing. Rather, the self-loathing some of these parents have developed—thanks largely to a society that enjoys flagellating its gay members—has permeated the relationships they have with their children. In some cases, they are unable to be close or honest with their kids because they are living a lie themselves.

Many of our contributors went through a great deal of personal pain to write these essays. Most of the writers had never before discussed—or, often, even thought to themselves—how having a gay parent shaped their world view, altered their value system, or helped them deal with issues of sexuality. Coming to terms with these issues was by no means a simple method; it catalyzed some serious discussions with their parents and friends. Some contributors found the process too difficult and decided not to participate. Others forged ahead and made some exciting discoveries about themselves and their families, as their essays illustrate.

Our goal in this anthology is not to show how families with gay and transgender parents are "just like everyone else," if "everyone else" refers to that illusory middle-class, straight white model of the nuclear family. Rather, we sought out essays that revealed the amazing diversity of experience among people with gay, lesbian, and transgender parents, a diversity we believe is reflected in the multiple family structures of today's society and includes gay and straight single parents, grandparents raising grandchildren, gay couples, and unmarried heterosexual couples. All of these families face the usual issues that come with raising a child; in addition, we found many common themes running through these essays, which show the particular challenges and rewards of growing up as the children of gay, lesbian, and transgender parents.

We hope this book will speak to these children in the United States today, as well as to a much larger audience eager to understand the consequences of changing family life. Significantly, that larger audience of readers will be allowed a glimpse into the real lives of these families—lives that are neither self-exploitative nor outlandish enough to end up on tabloids and television talk shows. Finally, and no less important, the members of these families will at last have a strong literary voice to speak about an experience long ignored or denied.

---

*We do not mean to exclude bisexual parents and their families from our discussion; certainly this anthology is meant for them as well. However, we felt it would be inaccurate to include "bisexual" in our book title, since we did not receive a single essay from a contributor whose parent self-identifies as bisexual. We believe there is a historical reason for this apparent omission: Before the 1990s, it was rare for individuals to claim a bisexual identity—the either/or binary mentality of both gay and straight society meant that people generally identified only as gay/lesbian or straight despite perhaps having relationships with both men and women. Since we sought contributors aged 15 and over, their parents all came from that era. We expect that many younger children today have parents who identify as bisexual, and perhaps they will write about that experience in the not-so-distant future.

OUT OF THE

ORDINARY

NOTHING TO ME

Sophia Gould

At eighteen, I stand on the steps at the art house cinema where my boyfriend works, watching the doors of Theater One. Usually, the moment the lobby clears, we'll find some corner, lean up against the wall, and kiss until a stray patron clears her throat at the counter. Then I'll blush, and my boyfriend will go serve popcorn. Once the patron is gone, we'll tangle up again until the credits run. Because of our displays, the manager has posted a sign that says, "No Making Out—or whatever you kids call it these days."

Today, as usual, my boyfriend wears black leather, and tight jeans, and I complement him in torn tights, a miniskirt, high lace-up boots. The Gay and Lesbian film festival is showing downstairs, and upstairs it's *Henry: Portrait of a Serial Killer*. I can hear the dialogue through the doors of both theaters, and I know we're clear for a good half hour, but I stay on the stairs.

"Come on down," my boyfriend calls sulkily from the ticket booth. I point to the sign, but the truth is I want to stay where I am. I enjoy watching the dykes filter in and out of the theater to order Jujubees and real Cokes. It feels like home. The audience members for the festival are mostly in their late thirties, sporting layered haircuts, beaded earrings, and Frye boots. If I squint, I could mistake them for my mother, as she looked eight years ago. Back then, she kept her hair above her ears and wore overalls or flannel, even home to our WASPy Christmas dinners, even among the pearls and angora of holidays.

My mother is married to a man now and has let her lesbian

friends drift away. That era of our lives is not something either of us talks about much. I haven't, for example, found occasion to mention it to my new boyfriend. Once upon a time, talking could have meant custody battles or social workers. Now, silence is an old habit.

Still, there's a comfort in looking at the women here for the matinee. For the same reason, I smile at the tattooed clerk who sells me my cigarettes and the purple-T-shirted band who clump together at pro-choice rallies. They remind me not just of the mother who raised me—now transformed into a microwave owner, a wife, a wearer of costume jewelry—but also of the dozens of women who were my surrogate mothers. Some were my mother's lovers, some just friends who, having lost their children to the courts or never having had any in the pre–turkey-baster decade, were drawn to me as a possible or temporary daughter.

The movie lets out, and I watch curiously but absently, half thinking of the kiss I'll get as soon as the lobby has cleared.

And then, there—nearly unchanged in the eight years since I last saw her—is Laura. Dirty blond, radiating competence, just as I adored her.

Panic. I flush. My chest constricts. I turn, then gallop up the stairs. Leaning over the railing, I watch, then pull away, then watch again until Laura—it *is* Laura—disappears out the door.

M y mother had known her in high school. They met again, both out lesbians, in the early eighties, and fell in love. It was long distance at first; Laura lived in Portland, Maine, and we were in Boston's Mission Hill. On our first visit to her apartment, I made a point of scattering the plastic army figures she gave me around every room. My mom thought it was cute.

"She's marking her territory," my mother said when I got up to join the grown-ups at the table, leaving a half-battled war in my wake.

"Pick those up," Laura said.

Something in her tone of voice made me do it. New lovers, in my previous experience, would indulge me, following my mother's lead. I could go to bed when the grown-ups did, watch late movies, and skip school to make up sleep. My mother believed ice cream could be dinner on occasion. But, as I began to learn, Laura believed in health food and rules. She was an activities director during the summer, and I could imagine she'd be happy with a whistle around her neck.

Rules were not always what I expected them to be. That summer, we went to pick Laura up at the ritzy camp where she headed the outdoors program. All the campers had left, and we scoured the cabins together, collecting the blue uniform sweaters the girls had abandoned, tubes of toothpaste, bars of soap, and other treasures that would see us through the lean winter.

"Taking what rich people leave behind isn't stealing," Laura explained to me. "They don't even think of this as wasting."

My mother and I shopped with coupon books in our hands, picking the green-banded no-name cereals over Kellogg's so that my father's meager support checks and the welfare would last the month. If the lines were long at the checkout, my mother was likely to dash back into the aisles and trade our butter for a jar of artichoke hearts or a bar of Swiss chocolate. On shopping night, we'd feast on the delicacy and then eat our toast dry for the next two weeks. When Laura moved into our home in September, the indulgences ended, but so did the sense of deprivation. She, too, had lived off slim earnings, but she had learned to stretch the checks into sufficiency. Unlike my mother, she was never tempted to sacrifice the end of the week for a Friday-night mimicry of wealth. If we needed more than we could afford, she'd find it for cheap, or free. Laura was the one who insisted we join the food co-op, and she did the volunteer work that kept our membership good. She planted vegetables in our yard, and the nearby Victory garden, and by the start of the school year, I was well trained in lifting rolls of toilet paper from public restrooms.

We were poor, and we stole little things—soaps, paper towels, pens, and sugar packets. My mother thrilled at these activities, filling her pockets with plastic stirrers she insisted we could make into a set of Pick Up sticks. Laura only shook her head slightly at this, but I could sense her disapproval. Later, leaving a small grocery, my mother pulled aside her coat to show us a pair of Chinese slippers that she had lifted, and Laura erupted. We should steal only from big stores or chain restaurants, she commanded, and only what we needed. My mother refused to take the slippers back and refused to pay for them, but after that, she left the stealing to Laura.

I didn't ask questions about these new rules, though they contrasted with the codes of my teachers, their *After School Special* morality. I already knew it was necessary, even right, to lie sometimes. When my teachers asked probing questions about my mother's roommates, for example, I was trained to feign ignorance. And my world was already one that acknowledged inequities. With my father, I saw first-run movies on weekend nights, and with my mother, I had to eat the stringy carvings of the jack-o'-lantern in a stew. When the kids at school called each other fags, I kept quiet, knowing that I could not argue, as long as my mother might be caught kissing a woman on a street corner, as long as she picked me up wearing jeans and a man's undershirt.

Though our thievery might, in complex terms, have meant something for the salary of the checkout clerks at Bradlees or the cost of necessities for other welfare families, Laura more than paid our debt by her involvement in the community. She and my mother joined the fight against a diesel power plant that a university wanted to locate in our neighborhood; perhaps they thought no one there would have the time or energy to object. And Laura was drawn to the kids in the neighborhood. She'd send stray kindergartners home at dark, help out with a dime for an Icee, bring out the wrench to loosen the fire hydrant on hot days. In Boston, 1980, there wasn't a single racially integrated Girl Scout troop until Laura became the troop leader of a multicolored band of Brownies from Roxbury and Mission Hill. On Wednesday afternoons, Laura would gather the kids of the poor lefties, the Hill, and the projects to cruise vacant lots for edible plants, which we'd roast over campfires between blown tires and rusted tin cans. And she never played favorites with me, even though I was the one who walked home with her. The other troop leader, Susi, was a nice married lady from down the block. I didn't know what she knew about Laura and my mother.

It took me a while to get used to Laura. She was tough, where my mother was indulgent. I had chores, suddenly. They would argue over whether I ought to clean my room.

"It's her space," my mother insisted. "She's the only one who has to live there."

But they were the ones who had to pick through my dirties to do laundry, and besides, Laura said, I'd have to take care of myself some day. I'd try, for a few days, to keep things neat, but when my room began to devolve to its old disorder, I'd wait until Laura was out of the living room before I opened the door on the mountains of toys and discarded clothes. I remember the shame I felt when she stepped over the mess to tuck me in and the way I'd make excuses for the crumpled papers and spilled juice: a social studies report, too tired, I promise I'll clean it in the morning. She looked, shook her head slightly, and reminded me I wasn't the only one who lived in the house. Naturally, I went to my mother when I wanted something. If I came home with a scrape from the playground, I knew which of them to find to show the wound to. Laura might know the proper first aid, but my mother would let me hold the iodine-soaked cotton to my own skin, would hold my hand and hush me as I cleaned the cut.

The second summer they were together, Laura got a job at a camp closer to home and brought me with her. It was a Campfire Girls facility, and most of the kids were from the North Shore, working-class, Catholic. They must have assumed Laura was my mother, and I suppose I let them. The rules were different at the camp. For example, Laura told me, I ought to be careful about my language. And I was, substituting "sugar" for "shit," the way I'd heard my grandmother do. And, I thought wisely, replacing "fuckin' " with "friggin'." The latter, however, turned out to also be considered a "swear" in North Shore circles. "Ooooh," one of the girls tattled, "Sophia said a swe-ar."

I was sent to the office of the camp director—Laura—for punishment.

"Well," she told me, winking. "I guess you'll have to be stuck in the office with me." She gave me one of the Popsicles that winning teams got in the color wars, and she made sure my mouth was clean of its orange mustache before I returned to my group.

I first began to think of Laura as one of my parents toward the end of that summer. Camp ended a few weeks before the start of school. Temporarily rich from her summer earnings, Laura took my mother and me on a canoe trip in Maine. While we were drifting during a lunch break, I took a bite of one of the green peppers we'd bought in the supermarket, and instantly my mouth was on fire. I was leaning over the boat, trying to swallow the river, by the time they realized what had happened.

"Jalapeño," my mother said, laughing at my red faced sputter.

It was Laura who handed me the chunk of oily sun-baked cheddar cheese, knowing the grease was the only thing that could neutralize the chile heat. And Laura waited until I laughed before she, too, cracked the smile that must have been pulling at her lips when I was choking down the river water. Laura's severity did not mean unkindness; for the most part, it meant the opposite, a form of affection. Unfamiliar—perhaps uncomfortable—but sincere.

Laura figured out how we could have enough money and things to survive, even if she did it unconventionally. She could fix whatever broke, and she contrived recreations for me that had somehow or other felt out of our financial reach before. But most of all, I think, she brought order to our scattered lives, an order I would need in the year to come. I made a habit of cleaning—or at least tidying—my room before I went to my father's on the weekends. I'd leave the laundry, in two separate piles, outside my door, and it was always clean by the time I returned. If Laura didn't come in with my mother to say good night, I'd call for her. They were my parents, both of them, at least on the weekdays.

The whole fall, I made my mother serve meal after meal of Uncle Ben's Long Grain & Wild Rice. If I saved a certain number of box tops, I could get a Coleman canoe for three hundred dollars, an amount I had nearly saved from birthdays and Christmases in my bank account. It was a brand-name prepackaged food that must have meant sacrifices for my mother, too, but she never let on. That Christmas, I gave Laura a beautiful green canoe. She took me into her lap and thanked me, then began to explain that we couldn't afford it, that she'd have to return it. I could feel my eyes burning. My mother tapped her on the shoulder, and they slipped off into the other room. I heard whispering and looked at the unopened packages with my name on them, trying to be excited. When they returned, Laura was smiling.

"Thank you, Sophia. It's a wonderful gift. We'll canoe in it till we're all old ladies."

When Laura went to make the coffee, my mother told me in a soft voice that she'd explained to Laura how the canoe would pay for itself, making up the cost of rentals in just a few years. Then she laughed.

"No, really, sweetie. She's keeping it because you gave it to her. Because she loves you."

In my memory, that was the day we were closest, most a family. My mother brought out her gift, three different-sized oars, which I had not been able to afford, and we climbed, one at a time, into the canoe, and mimed paddling down the river, while the other two steadied the boat on the scratched wooden floor.

Perhaps my mother sensed already, that Christmas, that whatever they whispered in the kitchen was the map of the end to come. But I was a child, and I could not read in these signs a possibility of an end. In a way there is no word for, I had also fallen in love with Laura. I had chosen her as my parent, chosen to take her rules as my own. But I had never chosen the risk of losing her. I assumed that, loving her as I did, she would stay forever. We would really canoe, gray haired, in the new boat, long after it had cracked and been repaired. Maybe I understood that my mother and Laura might split up. After all, my mother had left lovers, her husband, before. But Laura had become my parent and parents do not leave their children—after my father and mother divorced, he was still in my life, on weekends and holidays. I was ten years old; I never imagined that someone I loved might leave me, too.

DESPITE THE EFFORTS OF my mother's and Laura's group, construction began on the diesel power plant. From the top of Mission Hill, we could see the outline of smokestacks, growing higher almost daily. Watching it one night, Laura and my mother began a quiet debate of words I didn't understand, quick spelling out of letters I would lose track of before they formed sentences. When I asked what they were talking about, they both hushed, but after I went to bed, I heard their angry muffled voices from behind their bedroom door.

One night, when I was at my father's house, my mother and Laura went to spray-paint the community organization's symbol—a white elephant—on the walls of the university club. A witness phoned the police, who arrived midway through the painting and packed everybody roughly into the paddy wagon. My mother was the only one who spent the night in jail, the suspected driver of the getaway car, our Chevy van. The witness claimed she had watched my mother for a full three minutes and could make an identification—which, in legal terms, meant my mother could face eight years in jail.

They told me none of this. I watched the two of them bicker as they scrubbed every crevice of the car clean. No one asked me to help. When the doorbell rang, Laura would jump to get in my way, then eye our caller through the peephole before she'd slide the door open a crack. My mother told me I was no longer to answer; there had been a crime in the neighborhood (but there had always been crimes). I knew something was wrong, but I could tell by their silences and awkwardness, by the growing tension between them, that I shouldn't ask.

A month or so later, a group of women of my mother's height and coloring gathered in our apartment in the early morning to struggle into straight clothes, suits and lipstick, and accompany my mother to the police station for the lineup. The primary witness pulled the one woman in jeans from the group, a woman not my mother. Photos of the event showed officers without badges, twisting demonstrators' arms. The organization threatened a countersuit, and my mother got off.

But the events had taken their toll. My mother and Laura's arguments would already be in progress when I got home from school. A silence might fall for half an hour or more, while Laura walked around the block, but she'd return, pick up a grocery receipt, and circle each purchase she considered unnecessary. One afternoon, my mother met me at the door and took me to a shopping center, where we tried on ridiculously expensive headbands, patterned in red, purple, and green. I put each one back.

"Choose anything you want. My treat," my mother said. "We don't always have to suffer." But she couldn't find one she wanted, either. When we got home, Laura was still out, and it was nearly midnight when she finally put her key to the door. I heard them talking sweetly to each other in the bedroom, and I hoped it would be all right, but the next day, they were fighting again.

As I remember it, Laura's voice stayed calm and low, as my mother's pitched into screams, but this may not be fair. It may not be true that Laura was always right in these arguments but I felt, miserably, disloyally, that I was on her side. It may have only been that I wanted her to stay. And I began to realize, she did not have to. That was the difference. My mother did, and I could afford to sacrifice my support of her. *Just be quiet*, I whispered, hoping somehow my mother would hear it through the closed door.

When they argued, I went into my messy room and shoved toys and dirty clothes in the closet, the dollhouse furniture under the bed. I picked up the last miserable sock, the last Monopoly piece, the last thing that might make Laura give up on me for good.

LAURA LEFT WITHOUT A word. She took the canoe and, absurdly, ran off with Susi, her Brownie troop co-leader. My mother took me to an ice-cream shop and tried to explain over our banana splits. "I guess she just didn't care enough about us to say good-bye," she told me.

A month or so later, living in a new apartment where the memories were not so vivid for us, my mother found a note on the windshield of the van. She read it and ripped it up. When I asked her what it said, she told me it was from Laura. She wanted the rest of her stuff back.

> A few weeks pass, and I tell my father the story of seeing Laura at the movie theater.
>
> "Why didn't you talk to her?" he asks.
>
> "She left us," I say, and it's in my ten-year-old voice, long-lost self.
>
> "You know," he says, "She tried to see you. She called me a few times, I guess it must have been after their breakup, and said she wanted me to arrange a meeting between the two of you. She said your mother wouldn't let her see you."
>
> "And you didn't tell me?"
>
> "Sophia," he says, "I had no idea what the story was. I couldn't get involved."
>
> It is impossible for me not to wonder what the note on the windshield said or whether Laura had taken the canoe not because it was a nice boat but because I'd gotten it for her.

Years after that night in the movie theater, I became involved with a woman and on one of our first nights together, told her the story of my mother's relationship with Laura and my loss. Though my romance with this woman was short-lived, it opened the story for me again, and I began to search for Laura. I looked in the phone book for her very common name and penned a short, safe letter:

> *Dear L. Brown: I have taken your name from the phone*
> *book because I am in search of a person of the same*

*name. If the following description doesn't match yours,
please disregard this letter. My name is Sophia Gould. I
am looking for a woman named Laura Brown. She was
my Girl Scout troop leader in Mission Hill and a good
friend of my mother, Susan Patrick. Laura meant a great
deal to me. I am nineteen now, a student at Columbia
University. If you recognize these details, please write me
back at the above address.*

I made forty copies and shipped them to all of the L's, Lau-
rens, Loris, and Lauras in the Greater Boston Area. But she
could have been in San Francisco, or upstate New York, or back
in Maine.

I waited. A few weeks later, I got a letter in the mail:

*Dear Sophia: I remember you and I would very much
like to talk with you, but I have to ask that you not let
your mother know. I understand you may not feel comfortable doing this, but I can't have her in my life again.
Fondly, Laura*

I was fighting with my mother, and it didn't seem like an
unreasonable request. I wrote Laura back. But I never sent the
letter. A few months later, I wrote her again. I never sent that
letter either.

I COULD HAVE MAILED those letters. I have imagined coffee
dates, an exchange of photographs. It ought not to have been
difficult. And yet, eight years have passed since I received
Laura's letter. And I still haven't replied.

Why? I think of the sensation of being eighteen, of standing
on those stairs in the theater. The physicality of my response.
That is the beginning of the answer. I loved this woman, and
no matter what the real story is about her departure, the silence
I maintained over those years in some way must have frozen
my reaction. The letter, stamped and addressed, was kept from

the mailbox by a ten-year-old who'd been left without a good-bye.

I feared awkwardness, of course, or that she might not have missed me: a sterile exchange between two adult strangers who have little in common.

But it is more complicated than that. There is no paradigm for this love, this loss. When my mother's girlfriend left without a good-bye, there wasn't even a way to think about it. It became a heat in my adolescent chest, a sputtering lie to my boyfriend, an unmailed letter.

We know what these words mean. *Mother. Daughter.* And we have ways of understanding the separation of one from the other. To that loss, we would automatically ascribe unbearable devastation; we would expect far-reaching psychological consequences. Imagine if that loss had to be a secret, essentially unspeakable or haltingly revealed to a few trusted intimates. I have an affinity for TV movies about adoptees reunited with birth parents. I have a strange pattern of loving men whose fathers left when they were young.

No, it is not the same. And that's the problem.

And then there is the question of my real mother. Our peace has been hard won, as perhaps it is in all mother-daughter relationships, but it feels stable. What would happen if Laura confirmed my father's memory, my speculations? How can I account for the moment when my mother tore that paper in front of me? My mother was perhaps the only person who understood what it meant for me to have Laura gone. And, perhaps, she allowed me to believe that I'd been left as she had been.

An adult now, with my own history of romantic losses, I try to imagine what it might have been like, in those desperate days after I have had someone leave me, to also have a child. When one lover left me, I drove by his house to watch the lights in his windows—the smallest approximation of the intimacy I'd lost. And I sobbed, loud gasps, mucous-mouthed and ugly in my desperation. I drove through red lights on the way home.

When I think of my mother, in the days after she lost Laura,

I try to imagine a child in the passenger seat beside me that night, at that moment when I felt most abandoned.

And my mother, too, was working without precedents. How do you explain my loss to me? I am ten years old; I know nothing about the way adults love and leave. You can't write a note about it to school. You've been left in the worst way, for someone else, and suddenly, without warning. The end was so bitter that nine years later, your lover will write me that she cannot have you know we are in touch. You take me for ice cream. You protect me from the details, as you did with the arrest, believing this will save me somehow. Perhaps, when it comes time to answer my questions, you borrow the vocabulary from your own loss. Perhaps you say, "She left *us* without saying good-bye."

Of course, there is more to it than that. There might have been other, better ways. I might have sent the letter, but I didn't. We must create our own rules for such moments, and we are bound, sometimes, to fail.

IN MY ADULT LIFE, I have become a fiction writer, and the story I keep trying to write is this triangle, mother-daughter-lover. Now, the project has become a novel-in-progress, but at 175 pages, I still don't know how the mother will explain herself or what will happen when the daughter finds the lover. But in the fictional recounting, the girl gets to see her mother's lover leave. The girl wants to go with the lover. The lover won't let her: "I can't. I am nothing to you. Your friend, that's all."

What I mean by "nothing" is not the common usage, "You are meaningless to me," but rather that there is no name, no legal designation for that relationship. But the confusion of the ordinary meaning with my intended one is important: the relationship being unnamed, it became nothing.

The dedication will be to my mother, who stayed, who could stay. But I imagine myself someday finding Laura once again, showing up at her door unannounced, and handing her the galleys. "Read this," I'll say. "I wrote it for you."

MY FATHER'S EYES

Tristan Taormino

People say I have my father's eyes. The truth is, I have a lot of him in me—the sensitive Irish skin; dark hair that gets peppered early with salt; sharp teeth and an even sharper tongue. When I look in the mirror now, I always see him. Not the way he looked in the end, but the way I want him to look in my mind forever. I have this black-and-white picture of him, an old headshot from his acting days, and he was definitely matinee idol material. Even when he started going bald way too young he was attractive. And it was always his eyes people were drawn to first; they told everything about him. They never lied to me, never pretended, never disguised the truth. They were eyes full of love, desire, curiosity, confusion, mischief, sorrow, anger, and hope.

But I don't actually have his eyes. I think people tell me that so they can say they see the family resemblance. No, I don't have my father's eyes. He had bright blue eyes, blue that sparkles at you. Blue reflective glass that goes deep inside you and shows you who you are. I can see how my mother fell in love with him.

She has blue eyes, too, but they're calmer, more subtle. Different than his. As the child of two blue-eyed people, I, strangely, don't have blue eyes. Something about chromosomes and recessive traits. My eyes are no particular color, never the same color each time you see them. Sometimes they are pale, mossy green that turns brighter when I cry. Mostly they seem to be gray. Gray like steel beams or a smoky-colored cat. Gray like those days when you just want to stay inside under the covers.

I inherited not so much my father's eyes as his way of seeing. He's seen the projects in Red Hook, stern Catholic school nuns in black and white, army barracks in olive drab and mud brown. The red lips of Judy Garland in the restored version of *A Star Is Born*. The pink sequins of a drag queen's dress. The creamy color of semen on a stranger's stomach. Which is like the color of his skin. And mine.

His eyes shine images of Brooklyn summers, classroom punishments, basic training, and Hollywood movies like an old film projector on a bright white wall. It's like looking through a child's Fisher-Price View-Master, each image slightly blurry no matter how much light there is, each one framed with an old-fashioned white border. Sometimes the stories he tells are like looking through a kaleidoscope, repeated shapes and colors, mixing together differently each time I look. Making new patterns out of old ones, with memories of Coney Island beaches, Irish Catholic Brooklyn weddings, dinners with plenty of pasta and dysfunction.

Like so many gay men of his generation, he grew up in an openly homophobic family and was acutely aware of the gay-bashing culture around him.

The stories my father told about his mother were unbelievable—her fits of uncontrollable rage, her evil, sadistic methods of "discipline," recurring scenes of craziness and crying. In retrospect, I think she was probably manic-depressive—all the signs were there—but of course there was no awareness of mental health in that family. She was seen as domineering and moody, but never diagnosed with any psychological disorder. My dad and his mother disowned each other when he came out, and they never spoke again. I never met her. She died a year after he did.

"Fags are sinners, fags are perverts, fags are bad" was drummed into his head like an unyielding techno song. He took pleasure in his sexual adventures with other boys in his Brooklyn neighborhood but felt forced to hide his pleasure, deny it, hate it. He met other men like him in the army, a perfect homoerotic environment, but still felt forced to remain closeted. He took comfort in the arms of sexy strangers found in restrooms, movie theaters—found in secret. I believe he married my mother in a complex web of emotion: They truly were in love, and in 1960s suburbia, when you were in love, you got married. But I also think that marrying her was an attempt to escape his desire for men.

Movies were his other great escape, from pain to a world of love and drama. He had a fantastic crush on Montgomery Clift and identified with him in his closeted torment, his tragic star quality. And he thought he was a hunk, of course. I have a photograph of Montgomery Clift and Elizabeth Taylor on the set of *A Place in the Sun* hanging above my living room couch (which was my dad's living room couch). The photograph reminds me of his obsession with Montgomery, and it reminds me of the two of us: the way Liz Taylor looks, young and happy, and the way Montgomery holds her arm, gently, but deliberately. The old Hollywood of glamour and love.

MY FATHER'S PAST IS my legacy. I am a post-Stonewall baby who grew up in a time of more queer visibility, acceptance, and pride than my father could ever imagine when he was my age. And I had direct access to a gay and lesbian community through him. His was a queer world. So much of what we enjoyed together—listening to old Judy Garland albums, watching videos of the Divine Miss M in concert, showtunes and musical theater—was, to me, stuff my dad loved and I grew to love. It was only later, when I came out, that I realized his pleasures were also the typical tropes of gayness, but to me they were never clichés because they meant so much to him. Today, my own music collection is very queer, and very influenced by my father. Madonna, the Pet Shop Boys, and the Smiths sit alongside Stephen Sondheim, Betty Buckley, and Barbra Streisand.

I also had the opportunity as a teenager to live in Provincetown, Massachusetts, a bonafide gay mecca. A typical child of divorced parents, I lived with my mom and saw my dad for holidays and school vacations. When I was fifteen, I spent the whole summer at my dad's. I got my first job then, working at a leather shop, and spent my free time hanging out with drag queens and being crushed out on a bike messenger named Nina. I remember grinning a lot whenever she made deliveries to our store. She had muscles and jet black hair and looked like a tough tomboy all grown up. It never occurred to me that my friends back home on Long Island weren't having a summer like mine. It was a summer when Lola, a transvestite, taught me how to wear perfume. I wore perfume for the first time. She picked out the same scent that she wore—spiced apples and vanilla. It was a summer of lesbian potluck dinners and five o' clock tea dances at the Boatslip.

It was a summer of walking down Commercial Street hand in hand with my father. In my memories, we are dressed in some hip outfits on our way to see Jimmy James at the Pilgrim House. Jimmy James was close friends with my dad; he was a performer who impersonated Marilyn Monroe. They called it "female impersonation," but it was really more than that. Jimmy was the most exciting, most glamorous person I knew. Unlike the tired queens with cheap shiny dresses who couldn't even lip-synch very well, Jimmy sang Marilyn's songs and talked to the audience in her voice. And his nightly transformation was magical. When I saw him during the day, he was always cute and perky and witty. When he got himself in that peach-pink sequined dress, blond wig, and diamond bracelets, he *embodied* her. She was gorgeous and sexy and naughty and brash, and I wanted to be her. Not the Marilyn I'd seen in *All About Eve* with my dad, not the Marilyn on posters and T-shirts everywhere. I wanted to be the Marilyn that Jimmy was.

I also spent the summer watching my dad cruise other men on Commercial Street. He'd stop to flirt with some guy or another on the way. I can still see him moving his hands when he talked, fingering a guy across the ribcage, looking him right in the eye. It never felt that strange to see him with men, and even that first summer in P-Town, no one told me my dad was gay. They just assumed I knew.

I remember sitting at his kitchen table one afternoon with the younger brother of one of my father's friends. His name was John, but everyone called him Boomer, and his brother was a gay priest. "So, what do you think about your father being gay?" Boomer asked matter-of-factly.

It all came together at that moment in my head. *Right,* I thought, *my dad is gay. Of course. My dad is gay.* Because even through all the male roommates, the absence of any women lovers, his impeccable taste in clothes and decorating, it just didn't occur to me that my father was gay. And I was a pretty savvy fifteen year old. There was never any moment with either of my parents which began, "Honey, I need to tell you something . . ." But my mother had gay friends whom I adored, and it seemed perfectly fine that my dad was gay. Besides, he was not a typical father to begin with, regardless of his sexual identity.

MY FATHER WAS AN overwhelming source of love and encouragement throughout my life. He had the advantage, of course, of being a part-time weekends-and-vacations dad; when I visited him, I was usually on break from school or it was a holiday. He lived in many different cities—Boston; P-Town; Seattle; Portland, Oregon; and Portland, Maine—which meant lots of exploring new places for me. There was always plenty of shopping and good food, going to the theater, watching movies, and seeing friends. Unlike with my mother, there was little or no arguing about money, curfew, friends, rules, or setting limits, because that wasn't really his job. His job was simply to love and entertain me, and he did both splendidly.

There was a recurring, unspoken ritual my father and I had, which is one of my most treasured memories. When I packed for a visit with him, I always brought my best clothes, the hottest outfits, something brand-new I bought just for the trip, just for him. The first morning I was there, I headed for the bathroom, showered, primped for a long time, then dressed for him. I emerged from the bathroom, strutted into the kitchen or living room, and stood there in front of him, poised for his approval.

Without missing a beat, his eyes followed my body into the center of the room, lit up with glee, and he bellowed in a loud, expressive voice: "You look fabulous!" He'd say how much he loved my dress or ask where I got the shoes, and elaborate on his appreciation. It was my moment to shine, to be the beautiful object to him. It was our moment. I relive those times now with lovers, dressing up, anticipating the moment when she will arrive at my door or I will emerge from my bedroom, and she, usually a handsome butch, will survey every inch of me, drink me in with her eyes, smile, and say, "You look incredible." Sometimes, she'll even say, "You are beautiful, little girl. Come here and sit on daddy's lap."

My father loved to hold my hand in public. He loved me, wanted to show the world his affection. I used to think it was weird; I mean, no one else's father I knew held his daughter's hand so much. But I grew to like the hand-holding, especially as I got older. We were sometimes mistaken for a May-December romance, but, more often, people noticed that I was his spitting image. Even then, I think we still looked like we were in love. He'd take my hand in his, kiss me on the cheek, tell me a funny story, and I was completely content to walk down that road with him forever.

MY FATHER WAS MY power femme role model. He was always in charge, on top, running the show. His candor and assertiveness appealed to me; you always knew how he felt about something. He knew what he wanted and went for it without a trace of ambivalence. Even when he was diagnosed, he was clear in his living will that he didn't want to suffer. "I want the morphine drip," he used to say over and over: "Give me that morphine drip." Now, my father was not low maintenance by any means, and you could say he had some, well, *control issues*. But he pulled off that desire for control with warmth, grace, charm, seduction, and lots and lots of panache. He wasn't nelly or flamboyant in the way some of my favorite gay boys can be, but he wasn't the butchest boy around either. He was a subtle combination of aggression and compassion, dominance and emotion, flirtation and cool distance.

He was also more of a feminist than any of my radical activist girlfriends and more of a nineties man than any of my sensitive-type boyfriends. He was a mouthy, opinionated political beast and a fiery fighter for justice. Even when he got sick, he was still fighting to get the United Way to offer domestic partner benefits to its employees. He had remarkable radar for bigotry, double standards, and misogyny. He didn't learn about feminism in college; he figured it out in life. He saw inequality and oppression and took notice, gave it a name, tried to make sense of it. We used to have conversations that went on for hours about politics, equal rights, justice. He loved to hear about the trouble I was causing on campus, the marches I went to in Washington, the Queer Nation demos. Both my parents taught me to stand up for what I believe in and supported my activism; my father always challenged me.

My father made me the girl I am today—one who likes anonymous sex, show tunes, and well-dressed men. But my father passed on his wounds to me, too. I never thought there could be so much anger and sadness and rage inside one man. There was always lots of yelling and screaming and fighting with him. Slammed doors, frequent fallings out. He was so dramatic, always. And he is partly responsible for the drama queen I am today. Nothing was ever easy with him, and it was always intense and emotional. He was relentlessly honest about everything, and not always in a positive way. And while he was very serious about his relationships with people, they were always highly charged and overwhelmingly intense, and they often came to destructive ends. I believe that my father, like his mother, was manic-depressive or had some other mental illness and lived for years undiagnosed. His highs were quite high, and his mania manifested as fits of rage that were some of the scariest times I spent with him. When he got sick, there was some talk about putting him on antidepressants, but his moods were already altered by all the AIDS drugs he was on; there was really no point.

I WANT MY FATHER'S hand holding mine again. The last time I held his hand was at his bedside. He was incoherent, barely conscious. He couldn't talk anymore, only cringe to tell me— his only daughter—that the pain was getting unbearable. I'd press the button, and when the morphine kicked in, we'd watch the tape of Barbra in Las Vegas, and he'd smile. Sometimes he'd roll those blue eyes when the nurse he hated came by. Once, he squeezed my hand, and when I looked at him, he winked.

I want my father's eyes; I want to have those eyes now. Eyes that showed me what it was like before the big queer revolution. Eyes that sought out others like him in cities. Eyes that tried to make sense of the world before them. Eyes like mine. I want my father's eyes looking at me with love, with pride, with enchantment, the eyes of the one person who saw me the way I wanted to be seen, whose eyes showed me a beautiful, powerful woman.

I search for those eyes in crowds. On the subway, at parties, at that record store on Twelfth Street with the big musical soundtracks section. Sometimes I find a pair that shows me a smart-ass. Or a set that sees a soul in conflict with the struggle and the smile. Sometimes the eyes spy a girl who's all mouth and legs. I'm all those things, but I want the eyes that can see *that*. That look and love and understand. My dad was such a gorgeous combination of boy and girl, and I look for that blend everywhere. He knew and understood me in a way no one else ever has. He was my best friend, my mentor, my teacher. I was the object of his adoration and affection, and he was mine. He felt everything deeply, experiencing life by jumping right in. I am his spitting image, the charming queer girl to his boy. He instilled in me a belief that I could do anything I set my mind and heart to, the best gift of all. One that I hold close to me, one that drives me to do what I love.

WHEN THEY BROUGHT ME in to see him after he died, his eyes were open. Looking up at the ceiling. Far away. He had this red dot on the white of his left eye, the color of Judy Garland's lipstick. I drew my fingers over his eyelids to close them, like I've seen people do on television. But it didn't work. They stayed open. Stubborn. For the first time in my life, I couldn't see into him. And he couldn't see my eyes filled with tears; my eyes shining images of him—radical, loud, flirtatious, queer—like an old film projector on a bright white wall.

THE PROMISE OF DESSERT

Julie Diana Rawley

My great-great-grandmother bought the Hoosier cabinet in 1902 for a week's worth of groceries. When my mother broke her marriage vows, the cabinet was ninety-eight years old. It had moaned and rattled through many seasons in our big house, weighed down by our daily use, and though the Hoosier was worn and tired, smelling of dirty cinnamon, its solid pine frame did not bow. It had drawers within drawers and silent latches that exposed deep-set cupboards. My mother loved it and stored flour, rice, and baking spices in it.

My sister, Hannah, and I thought it was an ugly old green thing, the color of autumn leaves that never got word they were supposed to change. We gave it attention only when we sought a hiding place for some forbidden piece of food. I tucked cookies away so often that I inevitably lost track of some. When I was twelve I went searching for a goodie, allowing the cabinet to swallow my arm up to the elbow as my hand moved blindly along the back of the bread compartment until it landed on something sharp to the touch. I pushed a tin of wheat flour out of the way and discovered a dried-out brownie with jagged edges and a gray-green moss growing in the middle of it. Luckily, I'd found it before anyone else. As I quickly got rid of the evidence and sponged down the shelf, I pondered how chemically treated foods could last so long, unspoiled.

The Hoosier had not aged gracefully, and its thin coat of paint flaked away easily. We ridiculed my mother for choosing to keep the cabinet as part of the divorce agreement, but she insisted. She defended it the same way she defended the hour of meditation she'd added to her daily routine. Just as her daughters could not enter the bedroom while she was "breathing," so we could not separate her from the sentimental cabinet that she planned, finally, to refinish.

The Coast Guard transferred my father to Alaska while the three of us remained in California. Our new duplex was just four blocks from the high school I would be starting in the fall. My mother moved the Hoosier into a nook in the tiny dining room under the stairs. Hannah and I eyed it with disdain.

The doors to our new bedrooms and bathrooms were hollow and made no statement when we slammed them. I imagined that my strength would be enough to punch holes through the pressed wood. We were not encompassed or permanent or safe. We were not home.

My sister and I didn't object too loudly, though, to all the changes in our life, because the apartment complex was equipped with a sparkling blue pool. We spent our afternoons gleefully baking in the sunshine, listening to Miami Sound Machine and Cyndi Lauper, spending little time indoors. My mother had her share of friends over for dinner, and Hannah and I knew how to behave, at least until after the meal. We competed for the favor of mother's guests with a routine that lasted until they went home or until we were reminded of our bedtime. It started subtly. We went to our bedroom, clicked on the turntable, and played the *Footloose* soundtrack. I sang the lead vocals with glottal emotion, and Hannah chirped the backup *oohs* and *yeahs* while flailing her arms dangerously near bedside lamps and jewelry boxes. Once warmed up, we took our act downstairs and modified it for dishwashing. I scrubbed while humming through my nose and Hannah rinsed and dried as she tapped her slippers against the linoleum. At first, my mother and her friends tolerated us swooping in to lighten their work talk with jokes. They laughed lightly each time, then my mother would say, "Keep it down, please."

After the fourth or fifth interruption, her friends were no longer smiling at us. Our antics were getting to them; *good,* we would think, *maybe they'll leave.* My mother, however, contin-

ued to resist us, until we used our final plan of attack, the in-
cessant bickering that always made her pay attention.

"Mom, Hannah's been in my makeup. She's getting all the
eye shadows mixed together!"

"No I wasn't!"

"Yes you were, get off of me!"

We argued until she was forced to break us up. If we could
not mesmerize her at will, then at least we could make her
worry. Then maybe she would hear that we were really telling
her: *We can't survive without you.*

My mother would yell, "All right, girls, enough! Jean
doesn't want to hear your whining and neither do I. Now leave
us alone for a while." We retreated with our noses in the air,
as she confided in her friend, "They ignore me all day, come
home from school, I ask, 'How was your day?' they say, 'Fine.'
Then the minute I have company, they have to be the center of
attention." Hannah and I trudged off in separate directions with
our bruised egos. It was best for us not to be near each other
after such incidents. Our fights could become truly vicious once
each of us had seen our own neediness reflected in the face of
the other.

We never pegged Anne. When she visited, my mother offered us rare bait: ice cream sundaes and the right to watch
television in her room. We accepted her offer eagerly, and the
two of them slipped out to the store for their own dessert, leaving our dishwashing without audience. We resumed our private
pastime of artfully insulting each other, never consciously asking ourselves why they couldn't share the same ice cream we
already had in the freezer. When they returned, they sat on the
couch and talked about the small publishing company they
worked for, their intolerable coworkers, and other boring topics. I was very bothered at how softly Anne spoke. It seemed
that she didn't want to share anything with the world, as if her
thoughts were too precious, and only my mother had been
deemed worthy as audience. My mother giggled in a strange
new voice when Anne told her mysterious stories I couldn't
hear. I distrusted it all.

In the old days, when my parents had had friends over, they'd drunk gin martinis and wine and played games. One time my father galloped around the room, crying "Heigh-ho, Silver!" which made everyone laugh or yell out heartily. My mother never drank when she laughed with Anne because Anne didn't drink. Anne also listened to country music and we'd never had any family friends that liked that sort of thing. I didn't understand how Anne's insular, foreign world could interest my mother so.

By the time their visiting was over in the evenings, Hannah and I were asleep. I often had nightmares of an undulating red force field that surrounded me and felt dangerously unstable. Sometimes there were indistinguishable voices whispering and warning me of something I could not comprehend; sometimes there was only vast silence. My terror came in anticipation of being taken from that place, to somewhere far more menacing and unknown.

"You're dreaming of being expelled from the womb," my friend Jenni—who was unusually analytical for fourteen—exclaimed. "It's a reenactment of your birth."

I writhed under the covers and cried in my sleep, and one night I was awakened by my mother clicking the front door closed at 1:00 A.M. I called out to her, like I had when I'd wanted a drink of water as a little girl. She came to me after a few minutes with her warm hands that smelled of roses and cocoa butter and she whispered, "Why are you still awake?"

"I can't sleep, I had a bad dream."

"Just take some deep breaths, you'll be fine." She brushed my damp hair away from my face, and I tried to see her through the darkness.

"Did you go somewhere?" I asked.

"I just drove Anne home."

"Oh. Can we take a drive to the ocean tomorrow? Bodega Bay?"

"Not tomorrow, honey, Anne and I are going to an antiques fair."

"Antiques are boring."

"Okay, then. Go to sleep." She gave me two pats on the head and then moved toward the door.

"Please, can't we just go tomorrow?"

"Good night, Julie."

ON THE ONE-YEAR anniversary of our moving into the apartment, my mother sat me down on the bed to tell me something. The door to her bedroom was closed, and all the windows were shut. I sat at the foot of her bed and rolled my eyes.

"You've probably noticed that Anne has been spending a lot of time with us lately," she said.

It was true: I couldn't remember a weekend in the recent past when she hadn't been there. The Sunday before, Anne had arrived at the evening barbecue with a package of Smurf marshmallows for Hannah because my sister loved the cartoon so much. Like most people, Anne found Hannah irresistible. There was less than three years difference between us, but my sister's elfin nose, blond hair, and Elmer Fudd pronunciation of the *r* sound made her infinitely more adorable than me. Anne didn't bring me presents, not that I cared or anything.

My mother sat on her bed, leaned against her headboard, and told me about love in a too-soothing tone of voice that sounded like Glen, the therapist that she'd made me go see a few times. I didn't like him. He was always telling me to be supportive of my mother because her life was very stressful. He'd say, "What do you think it would be like to have two young girls that you suddenly had to raise all by yourself?" Once she'd made me go alone to see him and I'd sat in silence for forty-five of the sixty minutes. Only twice did he break the piercing hiss of the fluorescent lightbulbs and heating ducts in the room. I wondered if Glen and my mother were secretly in love. I knew he had a lot to do with my mother leaving my father. So my dad had a drinking problem. Was that a good enough reason to tear everything apart?

"Anne and I have grown to care about each other very much," my mother said. "Now, I don't expect you to understand how I feel. . . ."

"Okay, Mom, whatever. Can I go?" I felt an overwhelming need for Northgate Mall, for KFRC-AM, and Cherry Coke. The first time I had the new Cherry Coke was at the Regency Cinemas. It was me and Mom and Dad and Hannah and my best friend, Amelia, and it was a summer night and we went to see *Footloose*, and when we came out of the theater we were all laughing and snapping our fingers, even Mom and Dad.

". . . and I love Anne. Will you respect that, for me?"

I stared at her quilt. She liked women.

"Julie, will you look at me?"

I stayed with the quilt. Her hand touched my chin and tried to lift it up gently. I batted her hand away and looked past her.

"Just change! Just change back!" I screamed, and ran from the room.

I knew she was crying. *Good*, I thought. *I want her to be miserable. Maybe then she'll understand how I feel, and she'll take it all back.*

I went to the carport and sat down on our car's front bumper. It was my only private place, and I cried silently and heavily. She was ruining my life. Now all the beautiful, popular girls at Novato High with perfectly feathered hair would never accept me. They were all smoking Benson & Hedges Menthols 100s, and I had not yet mastered French inhaling. I kicked oily pebbles underneath the car. No one was gay in Marin County. No one's mother would actually choose another woman over her children. My nose was full and I had no tissue, so I tried to stop myself from crying but could not.

"DO YOU THINK THEY, you know, do it? And how would they do it?" Teresa asked me.

She was the only one I told at first. We were alone in the school bathroom, in the haunting quiet of third period. I breathed in fumes from ammonia and industrial pink powder soap, my eyes gleaming wet against my will as I tried to imagine my mother in Anne's solid arms. The moment the image came to me, I turned to the cloudy mirror above the dripping sinks. More makeup. I smoothed a peppy fuchsia shade over my lips, layer after layer, until they looked big and creamy, just like in the fashion magazines. Girls' lips were meant for boys to kiss, not for other girls. I wasn't crazy; everything around me, television, movies, and popular music, told me I was right. My mother was no longer well.

"Like, are they gonna get married?" Teresa was still peppering me with questions.

"I don't know, I don't know," I blubbered, my voice echoing through each and every graffiti-covered stall. "Just please don't tell anyone."

"Don't worry, and remember you can always come stay with me," Teresa said. She held me for a minute and let me cry into her moussed hair. Her hug was fragile, not firm like my mother's could be, but I tried not to think about it, and leaned on her.

BOXES OF FOOD BEGAN appearing in the Hoosier with Anne's name written over the label. Hannah and I weren't to touch the Raisin Anne, the Cream of Anne, or the Nature Valley Granola Anne. My grandparents lived an hour and a half away in the Central Valley, and when they came to visit, they never looked in the cabinet. They had no reason to look; my mother had not told them yet, and none of us were looking forward to that conversation. My grandmother was still convinced that my parents would eventually get back together.

A few days after my mother told me everything, my grandmother made her weekly phone call. I still felt venomous with anger.

"Hold on, Mom," my mother said, and then turned to me in my dazed position in front of the television.

"Julie, hang this up, I'm going to take it upstairs." I didn't answer her.

"Julie!"

I stomped to the phone and held it at arm's length while she climbed the stairs. I wanted to listen in once she picked up, but I knew she'd never be fooled.

I knew they were talking about me, about Friday night and

how I'd come home smelling of booze. I turned off the television and went to the Hoosier for an apple fritter I'd stashed away two days ago on the highest shelf. It was a little crunchy on the outside, but it still tasted good. Had my mother no idea what it meant to be a teenager? Why couldn't she understand that drinking was what everyone did before dances? I could hardly believe her story of how she'd never touched alcohol or cigarettes until college. Besides, that was her life, not mine.

"Julie, Grandma wants to talk to you," she called from upstairs, and I buried the rest of my fritter at the bottom of the trash.

"How are rehearsals coming along for the musical?" Grandma asked. She knew how to engage me. I knew that I was more like her than I'd ever be like my mother.

"I love it," I said. "No one in the cast can believe that I'm only a freshman. They're all juniors and seniors and they think I'm so mature for my age."

"You are mature, Julie. You're a very smart girl. And you can be doing a lot at home to help your mother. Try not to argue with her so much. I was a teenager once, I know how confusing that can be. But try to remember that you've only got yourself to worry about. Your mother's got herself and you girls."

I wanted to cry, *There's something she's not telling you!* But I couldn't. I wanted to say, *I'm on your side, I want Mom and Dad to get back together, too!* But I didn't.

I said, "I'll try."

That next weekend my grandparents came to town and took us out to dinner. Hannah and I loved being their guests; they let us order whatever we wanted, even dessert. My mother ate the food they purchased without protest, but she answered their questions vaguely.

"Did I tell you about our new minister? A woman?" my grandmother asked.

"Uh, I don't think so," murmured my mother.

"Well, she's new to Elk Grove, and she thinks she can change traditions without any regard for those of us who grew up in that church."

My grandfather said, "That woman doesn't know who she's dealing with here." He winked at my sister and me, and my mother erupted with a laugh that was too automatic. It was her fake laugh that I was growing used to. It was replacing the real laugh that she reserved for the woman across town whose name was a four letter word. I sat there across our spumoni ice cream and watched her lie to her parents. She didn't care about any of us anymore.

THE FOLLOWING MONDAY I came home to an empty apartment and decided to take advantage of a few precious hours alone. I picked the newly installed lock on my mother's bedroom door and I hunted. I looked for whips, leather underwear, straps, buckles.

Under the perfectly made bed I found winter boots and acrylic blankets that snagged on my uneven fingernails. In the closet I found a box of sewing notions: pearly buttons, safety pins, and unused clothing labels embroidered with Hannah's name and my own. Hanging neatly were easy-to-care-for blouses, pastel ties, a holiday vest, and an assortment of corduroy slacks. I went to the bureau and opened and closed the drawers violently. I spotted a box leaning against the dresser that caught my eye.

The Hitachi Magic Wand was relief for tired muscles.

Yeah, right.

I inspected it, not really knowing what I hoped to find. I turned it on and it vibrated. I turned it off. I rolled it in my hands. I checked the clock and took it to my bedroom.

I'd learned about the pressure of the bathtub faucet a year earlier. My best friend, Amelia, had told me about it when she'd returned from summer camp. I'd mastered its flow along with the motion of my own hand, but this electrical thing was totally foreign to me. I feared that what I planned to do was dirty, but I couldn't ask Amelia; she, too, was a military brat and had moved to the East Coast a year ago. Six years of secret pacts and sleepovers had ended, and no one, not even Teresa or Jenni, had come near to replacing her in my high school life. I peered over my windowsill and saw the pool down there, blinding diamond blue. It was empty. The whole courtyard was empty. Just swallows cheeping with delight under the cool, shadowed eaves. I drew the window blinds, and my room became dark. My door was shut. It was as secret as I could make my world.

It felt clinical at first and it made noise, so I tried to cover it up by humming with the low voltage. I imagined lying underneath Jed Merritt. He'd said hello to me in the halls nearly every day for the past month. I laid back on my bed, relaxed, and heard him through the buzzing. He was whispering wonderful, unspeakable things in my ear, and I was swooning. I was half believing that a boy would really say such things to me. After the moments of feeling so alive, like the only creature on Earth, I sat up on my bed and turned the thing off. I parted two blinds and saw that the courtyard was still empty. The sun burst its way into my room, light rounding the walls. The massager that my mother had purchased lay lifeless on my lap. I tried to reconcile the image of her buying it, standing at the counter of a department store, taking money out of her big purse-for-all-occasions that was filled with Juicy Fruit gum, Stayfree pads, nail files, dental floss, and tissues. It was the same purse she'd carried during our annual school clothes shopping sprees in San Francisco. Those outings were as important to me as Christmas. She'd always given us cards full of confetti on our birthdays. As far back as I could remember, she'd set aside one night each year for a no-sleep televisionfest full of nachos, root beer floats, anything we could dream up. I couldn't imagine that my mother would ever want to do any of those things again unless Anne was there, too. I washed the massager and put it back in its box, just as I'd found it.

MY MOTHER FOUND A book askew on her bedside table and installed a better lock on her bedroom door. Summer approached in ribbons of heat that left me unable to see past my own outstretched hands. I spent all of my time at home in the pool. My sister liked to sun in the lawn chair and greet the neighbors that walked by: Bill, the manager with the glass eye; Leslie, the lady who belonged to the Rajneesh cult; and Bobby, the swinging bachelor who shined his motorcycle while wearing nothing but Speedos. I sat at the bottom of the deep end, holding the sides of the pool so I would not float to the top.

My mother was on our deck, pruning the tomatoes in a tank top that made her arms look muscular, like she might enjoy hauling bags of cement. She had just recently cut her hair shorter than it ever had been before. It was almost spiked. I held my breath longer and longer in the depths, but every so often I heard her call out to the others in the complex. How could they bear to be seen having a conversation with her?

On the last day of my freshman year I joined a group of graduating seniors for an all-night party. They had befriended me throughout the year, and that night they supplied me with all the wine coolers I asked for. I came home around 4:00 A.M. That morning I realized—to my great annoyance—that I had left my purse somewhere the night before. My mother, still agitated from my early-morning entrance, drove me to all the houses I could remember and waited while I knocked on door after door. Each time I returned empty-handed she muttered and wrenched the car into reverse.

"Do you remember anything?" she asked me. I turned the radio on, and she turned it off. "Do you worry at all about how this makes you look?"

"I don't worry about my friends."

"So they get blind drunk, too? They forget everything and make complete fools of themselves? You're better than that, Julie. I expect more of you."

I looked at her clenched hands on the steering wheel. "You're not being fair," I said.

"Oh, I'm being more than fair."

"No! You can do whatever you want with your life, but I make one mistake and I'm punished like a criminal."

"There's a difference, Julie. I'm an adult, and you are not, and there are some things that the law will not allow you to do, and as long as you live in my house you will obey the rules." I was so angry I figured the truth wouldn't matter to her: that I'd sat alone all night, on beanbags and couches with a bottle in my hand, watching my older friends disappear into bedrooms with grinning boys. I hadn't done what they'd done. I'd been safe. If I'd hurt anyone at all, I'd only hurt myself.

Not long after, she informed me that I would be moving to Alaska, to live with my father. "I can't handle you anymore," she said. "I just hope that your father can reach you."

"What about Hannah?" I asked.

"She isn't acting out like you are. I just feel helpless when it comes to dealing with you."

The truth, I knew, was that Hannah didn't reject her relationship with Anne. When my mother had told her about her new gay life, Hannah had said, "Mom, I don't care if you love a monkey, I still love you." My mother had thrown that in my face plenty of times. I thought she was shipping me off because I reminded her of how guilty and ashamed she ought to be.

Anne moved in less than a month after I was gone. Once I was settled into my father's military quarters on Kodiak Island, I auditioned for a community play directed by a short, graceful man named Michael Underbrook. He told me I was talented and cast me as the young ingenue in his summer production. Later, I stood in my father's garage, amid empty Coors cans and told him how excited I was. He congratulated me from under the hood of his race car and told me he was glad for me "even though," he said, "that Michael is as funny as a three-dollar bill." I didn't ask him how he felt about my mother being gay. I didn't imagine he'd have answered me while he was sober, and drunk, I feared he would say too much.

It was common knowledge in the Kodiak community that Michael Underbrook was gay. No one seemed to care, and, in fact, he was revered as an artist on the island. I watched him carefully during rehearsals and was perplexed at how normal he seemed. He didn't flirt with the men, and he paid no less attention to the women. He treated me like a niece, and his generous attention made up for the silence dominating my new motherless, sisterless home.

I wrote letters to California in a well-tempered voice, and I prayed my mother would read the difference in me. I got decent grades in school and I made friends. I joined the parties at the beach on weekends, but my dad was numb enough not to notice when I came home late. I wanted to convince my mother that I was a good daughter again, that I was ready to move back to California.

When I returned for a visit the following summer, and only a visit, as I was told upon arrival, I tried very hard to be pleasant and open. I told my mother about Michael Underwood and how much I had learned from him.

"And he's gay!" I announced, with bright eyes and a cheery smile.

She said, "Oh, yeah?" but did not say I could move back in with her.

When I got home, I discovered that the Hoosier had a new face. It had finally been stripped, painted white, and accented with pink pinstripes and green blossoms. My mother and Anne had transformed the apartment into a colorful museum full of antiques refurbished, varnished, and framed. Everything was tidy and fresh smelling. My mother was living amid history, but she'd learned to control the memory of it masterfully.

I tried to hide the disappointment and anger I felt in being replaced by Anne. I concentrated on all I had learned from knowing and working with Michael. It worked, sometimes.

I brought home a half pound of chocolate almonds one afternoon. I knew my mother wouldn't approve. I went to the Hoosier with the intention of hiding my treasure in the familiar crevices and coves as I had for years. But all the holes had been filled with new Tupperware and cereal boxes and craft supplies. My hands searched around invisible corners and I felt new, smooth interiors. Nothing was being hidden in there anymore. Hannah hadn't mentioned any of this to me when I'd grilled her on what had taken place in my absence. When she came home that day, I didn't ask her to explain. I put my chocolate inside my pillowcase. I supposed she'd found her own new hiding places.

I did not move back to California. I finished growing up in Alaska. I added red and blue throw pillows to my father's bachelor couch, inspired by the new decorations I found in my mother's house each summer. In my junior year of high school I cooked the entire Christmas dinner for my father and his fiancée, and my ham came out just right.

I went on to college, and when I was twenty-two, I shared a pot of coffee with my mother early one morning, before Anne woke up. My mother told me she thought I'd grown into a remarkable young woman. She'd told me that a million times in the letters she'd sent to me since the first summer I'd left for Alaska. I had a box in my Seattle apartment filled with cards from Easter and Thanksgiving and St. Patrick's and Valentine's and Independence Day, all signed the same way. "I'm very proud of you."

We buttered our scones and watched the early eastern light fill the sky and illuminate the blooming backyard.

"Anne and I are going to a dance tonight, for gay couples," she offered, gingerly.

"Good for you," I said, and smiled so she knew I meant it.

We were sitting in the dining room of the new house she and Anne had bought and filled with color and culture. I looked at the old Hoosier across the room, under the big windows, and realized I was no longer offended by it. In fact, I was surprised to find that I even liked it.

SEXUAL HEALING

Noelle Howey

It was just about my favorite game in sixth grade, second only to Hooker Barbie and Pimp Ken.

I sneak one of Mom's teddies—if possible, the gold one with snaps on the bottom—out of Dad's dresser (for some reason, she keeps them in his underwear drawer), take one of Dad's *Playboy* magazines from under an old copy of *Newsweek* in the linen closet, and lock the bedroom door.

I Scotch tape the shades to the window sill, glide on some cherry Lip Smacker and sky-blue eye shadow, stick the record needle on "Like a Virgin," and try to keep the teddy—about ten sizes too big for me—from falling off. I keep an ear out for Mom or Dad coming up the stairs.

"I know you want it," I whisper.

I crook my leg around the door frame and glide my crotch up and down against the edge. "Do it, like, hard," I growl, my hot breath forming small, moist circles on the wood.

I pretend the door frame is named Jake, and that he is a sexy, tall ninth grader who looks like the guy on the cover of the *Sweet Valley High* books. I try to get him to want me. It's sort of easy in that guys always want sex but hard in that guys like big boobs and I just have these little bumps that my friend who got her period in elementary school calls spider bites.

When I am ready to have sex with Jake, it feels like I have to pee, and I hold myself like when I have to go and can't unlock the door fast enough to get in the house.

Before I put everything away, I squat on the bathroom sink in front of the mirrored medicine cabinet and pout my glossy pink lips. I run my hands down my hairless legs, unsnap the teddy bottom, and arch my privates up toward the mirror, singing " 'Cause I'm a woman" from the Enjoli commercial, quietly so no one can hear. I grin and imagine the day, maybe in high school, when I'll wake up and look exactly like the femme fatale of my fantasies.

While I am playing, Dad is down in the basement, a place where all dads like to be. It's cold and made of concrete; there's a sawhorse, a tool box, and an extra fridge filled with Budweiser. He says he is working on a project. I assume it involves shellacking an end table. It doesn't.

My father has tucked himself in the windowless back room of the basement, the only place in the house he truly feels at home. He takes out the portable makeup mirror from behind the solvents, a cache of old dresses from under the camping equipment. He leans into the mirror, trying on a new pair of eyelashes. He slicks on Ruby Red Max Factor and puckers. When he hears a creak on the steps, he frantically starts unscrewing his jar of Pond's Cold Cream. It's just the cat. Exhaling, he slips into a green hausfrau number. He imagines himself done up in an apron, merrily folding the laundry for the whole clan. In the dim light of the basement, he can barely see his stubble or Adam's apple. He runs his hands over the padded bra, trying to ignore the stray chest hairs. This is ridiculous, he thinks. He needs another drink. Stoically, he wipes all traces of the cosmetics from his face. He goes upstairs and barks at me to get away from the TV because it's time for the PGA championship. When my mother comes home, he tells her he spent the afternoon finishing the end table.

M y father is a transgendered lesbian, a biological male who thought of his Y chromosome as a cruel cosmic joke and wanted, above all things, to become a female. Over the course of my teenage years he metamorphosed into a woman through exhaustive estrogen therapy, electrolysis on every last facial hair follicle, and sex reassignment surgery. But for both of us, the process of becoming a woman was more complicated than mere physical transformation. We didn't realize then that we would spend years unconsciously trying on and discarding different, and equally limiting, images of womanhood before we were able to create versions that fit.

I got a jump start on the whole woman thing, being born a girl in the summer of 1972. From the time I could gurgle, I embodied the sugar-and-spice nursery-rhyme image of girldom. I had the long golden Heidi braids, a toy chest overflowing with Mattel paraphernalia, and ballet-slipper wallpaper. To the bemusement of my former tomboy mother, I was as close to a stereotype as one could get. And I charmed the pants off everyone—except, unfortunately, my father.

He was raised in the testosterone-poisoned atmosphere of the fifties and spent much of his adolescence being mocked in school bathrooms because boys sensed his effeminacy. He learned that the only way to survive was to emulate his bullies, to swagger and scoff like a varsity letterman. It worked, superficially. He married my mother at twenty-four, right on schedule, and then glad-handed his way up the old-boy corporate ladder. By the time I was born, my father had fully fashioned himself into a Michael Douglas–John Wayne hybrid who strutted around the house in a leather jacket and mirrored sunglasses. He had even acquired all the requisite guy accessories: a sports car convertible, a clunky gold watch, a *Sports Illustrated* swimsuit desk calendar, and a major chip on his shoulder.

As far as I could tell, my father was cold, brusque—and normal. Most of the kids I knew loathed and feared their never-there, always-angry fathers. But I didn't want to settle for that; I craved his approval and longed for a connection. So when he came home, downed a few screwdrivers, and slowly eased into drunkenness, I would climb up on his lap to cajole a hug or an Eskimo kiss. If he was feeling affectionate, he might pat me abruptly on the head. Usually, he would squirm and complain that my head was blocking the TV. My mother always apologized for him. "He loves you but doesn't know how to express it," she would say. "Some men are like that."

These days, my father says she loves me with every phone call, in every handwritten birthday card. She can do that openly now that she has been untethered from her male body and, so she says, the cold distance she felt she needed to keep from breaking down and admitting who she was. I sympathize with the anguish she felt sitting there in that recliner, so paralyzed by self-loathing and terror that she could not embrace her own young daughter. But it will take me the rest of my life to truly understand why she couldn't find a way to express love for me while she lived in a male body.

I WAS IN NINTH grade when my mom dropped the news. In a halting, whispery voice she said that dad liked to wear girls' clothes and needed to move out in order to understand exactly what that was all about. I was predictably shocked. So is dad like Tootsie? Or Boy George? It seemed impossible that my dad could be anything but a tough guy. But oddly, I felt an enormous flood of relief rush over me. *So that's why he's such a jerk*, I thought, almost giddy with the revelation. *He's a freak. It's not me. I am not the problem.*

Later that week, my father took me out to lunch, still wearing his same guy clothes. I scrutinized him for any noticeable signs of femininity and found only that his nails were kind of long for a guy—way longer than mine were. Over cheeseburgers and nacho fries, he told me he wasn't just a transvestite, but a transsexual, which meant he felt he should have been born a woman. He said he had felt trapped in the wrong gender his whole life, and that's why he had so many problems communicating with me and my mom. He still loved us, but he couldn't live in a man's body anymore. I nodded. I didn't have any questions—yet.

Frankly, I was a little preoccupied. I had recently become aware that I was, in fact, hideously ugly and, to my embarrassment, had been walking around for at least a couple years under the delusion that I was still a cute lil' blond moppet. Not so. My skinny-rail body was underdeveloped, and my home perm hadn't quite worked out as planned. Between clothes shopping, trying makeovers at every cosmetic counter, and writing lists in my daily journal of ways to improve myself, I didn't have much time to think about my dad. At least that's what I told myself.

Truth is, I was terrified. I feared that if I paid attention to my father's transformation, I wouldn't be able to stem the inevitable tide of fierce emotions. Like many children of divorce, I saw my dad at lunch every weekend. He was still somewhat closeted, so he looked like a man. But each Saturday he would appear just a little more girlish. Maybe he would be wearing pedal pushers, or open-toed sandals. Sometimes his long fingernails were polished. Often now, he would sit with his legs crossed instead of wide apart, or gently dab the corners of his lips with a napkin instead of rubbing vigorously. His voice started to get a little squeakier and giggly, as though he had been sucking on a helium balloon. I tried to ignore the changes, but each one sent a visceral shock through my body. Watching my father week after week was like watching a film progress one frame at a time.

To my relief, no one else really seemed to notice. No waiters called him ma'am, no clerks gave him bewildered glances. Dad still drove his sports car and made the same six-figure income. The lack of serious, tangible change in my father's life allowed me to stay distant and view this little "transgender thing" as an odd diversion, a personality quirk with no real impact on our day-to-day lives. So I focused my energies on being a perfect student and burgeoning political activist, and, by my junior year of high school, into sex.

I lost my virginity with my boyfriend on New Year's Eve, 1988, at the age of sixteen. As we lay on his mother's quilt with a bath towel under us and I watched him scrunch up his face and grunt in a peculiar, pleasing way, I felt intensely female. Sex wasn't much physically, but the sweaty glee on my boyfriend's face gave me a sense of triumph. Giving him pleasure gave me a surge of power. Wow, I thought. I can make him want me.

From then on, I honed my seductress skills. Every few days

after school, I would excitedly change into my Victoria's Secret lingerie—a black teddy that, just like my mother's old lingerie, would barely stay on my body—and pose in various sultry, cinematic positions for my boyfriend's approval. See, I *am* a sexy woman, I would think, delirious with satisfaction. I would move up and down next to him, perfecting the technique I'd developed with the door frame. I felt so aware of my breasts, my legs, all the ways I could make my boyfriend's breath catch and his eyes narrow into lascivious slits. The intercourse was an afterthought, filled with panting and sweating and my suddenly remembering Algebra II homework.

Sex provided a powerful distraction from thoughts of my father. By the time my mom got home from work, I'd be tired, and impassive from the sexual calisthenics. I wouldn't want to talk about *howdoyoufeelaboutdad*. Instead, I put on a perky face and shrugged when she asked me how I was doing. "I'm great," I automatically answered.

THE FIRST CRACK IN my purposely indifferent teen exterior came when I saw my father fully dressed as a woman. She loped up the driveway sporting nautical wear from the Gap, with a mop of brown curls and pink lipstick. She looked like the quintessential PTA mom—no *Some Like It Hot* drag queen here. My God, I thought, she is really doing this.

Except for having suspiciously thick wrists, there was not a single sign that she was genetically a middle-aged man. I knew she had been having electrolysis treatments, and I had witnessed the purple bruises from the eye tuck and chin lift that briefly mottled her face. I also realized she had been on major hormones. But I had no idea how smoothly she could morph into a passable—even attractive—female. It scared me beyond belief. My stomach clenched when I saw her hairless arms, the small bumps on her chest. What hit me hardest, though, was spotting a thin Timex watch on her wrist where a chunky Rolex had been. My dad always wore that thick gold watch. Now it was gone, packed away in a box as though he were dead. I didn't say a word. I hugged her tensely and ran up to my bedroom to do homework.

I wonder now if my family could have used a mourning period. My mother and I could have dressed in black and sat in the living room, being fed cold cuts and pickle spears, recalling the time that my dad got drunk at Rick's birthday party or we got lost in Washington, D.C., and Dad swore until he turned purple. But instead, my mother and I believed our own rhetoric—that he was the same, only different, and that our family was still intact and loving, only divorced and just a little confused. We tried not to acknowledge that the change my father was making was more than cosmetic, and that even if it was ultimately for the better, it still entailed profound loss.

I saw my dad's new home on my first spring break from college. The two-story in a neighboring suburb was unquestionably Martha Stewart. Three of the rooms were painted mauve, fresh rose-shaped guest soaps lay in a cup in the bathroom, and everything was spick-and-span, as though she had just discovered housework. And in a way, she had, since the extent to which she participated in cleaning up until then was to lift up her legs while my mother vacuumed between the recliner and ottoman.

Beaming, she told me that she had taken up flower arranging in place of bowling—her guy obsession. Indeed, small vases of dried pink flowers sat on every tabletop on the first floor. One sat next to a plate of freshly baked chocolate chip cookies. The bile in my stomach rose as I walked from room to room. It seemed as though my father had liberated himself from his repressive masculinity to become a Nick at Nite mom.

A recently declared women's studies minor who proudly eschewed makeup and cut my hair butchy short, I was irritated by my father's apparently simplistic notion of what it meant to be a woman. I couldn't believe she would go through physical pain and risk the enmity of everyone she had ever known in order to act the role of domestic goddess.

In truth, much of my discomfort with feminine trappings came out of my own convoluted use of them. I still couldn't have sex without dressing up in lingerie or engaging in a strip-tease, even though I owned my fair share of feminist literature. And I would rather have died than tell my friends in the women's collective that feeling like a hot chick worthy of objectification was just about the only way I could get horny. I didn't know how to reconcile my own paradoxical desires, so I lashed out at my father about hers.

On the third day I was home, my father prepared yet another in a string of meticulous menus for me: mesclun salad and wild mushroom lasagna. The fancy food sent me careening over the edge. Halfway through dinner, I exploded. "This isn't what being a woman is all about, Dad," I informed her. "Look at me. I'm a real woman. I go on marches for choice, and sign petitions, and fight sexual harassment. You're playing house. You're reinforcing every single stereotype of what a woman is supposed to be, circa, like, 1956." My father sniffled—as she often did these days—and said she didn't think being a woman was all about housework and that I should give her a little more credit, thank you very much. She said she was trying some things out she hadn't been allowed to do as a man. Wasn't feminism about being able to choose the lifestyle that works for you? she demanded. "Well, yeah," I scoffed, "but *this* isn't what we mean by choice."

My father and I did not stay angry at each other; rather, our seemingly endless series of debates over whether transgenderism was inherently sexist or not drew us closer together. And over time, as I started to mellow and allow that maybe I could wear lip gloss and still be a card-carrying member of NOW, I began to understand that my father's innate desire to be a woman transcended all these arguments. Observing my father— once embittered and half drunk much of the time—bask in an almost Zenlike contentment even as her friends and family and work clients were drifting away made me realize the depth of her longing. I began to trust that what she was doing was essential for her happiness and probably even her survival.

When I was twenty-two, I accompanied her to Belgium for her sex reassignment surgery. It was an act of contrition and a sign that I accepted her decision to be the fullest woman she could be. She was white-knuckled with fright the night before the surgery. She paced around the hotel room, suddenly paranoid that her penis had become too small from the hormones and would not invert into a sufficiently deep vaginal canal. I felt for her but also was aware that such talk would make me sick; I threw up most of my dinners during our week in Brussels. I didn't realize just how much the surgery would reopen my own wounds about losing my father as a man.

Lying there in the hospital awaiting surgery, with Magic Marker indicating where the incisions would be made in her groin, my dad looked like a train wreck of genders: bald and breastless (she had removed her padded bra), but immaculately manicured. During the next several hours, as the doctor cut off her testicles and converted her penile tissue into a clitoris and vagina, I sobbed into her bed pillow until my throat hurt and my stomach tied in knots. For perhaps the first time, I realized that my old father was gone for good.

In the aftermath of the surgery, I fell into a deep clinical depression. Finally, I was grieving the death of a man I barely knew and didn't like but still loved. Moreover, I was lamenting the permanent loss of white-bread normalcy. The surgery made everything final: he was a woman, my parents weren't ever going to reunite, and no one would ever look at us like a standard middle-American family again. I threw myself into a new relationship in an attempt to save myself from total dismay. It didn't work. My boyfriend was subtly experimenting with gender-bending, growing his hair out and wearing women's cardigans. I couldn't accept it; to my own embarrassment, his long, soft hair and petite body frightened me.

Though I never said anything, I started fantasizing about him being taller or wider or meaner—the way a guy "should" be. My need to be the soft, pliable object of his gaze had transformed into something sinister and unhealthy. In the absence of a stern and neglectful father, I wanted my boyfriend to adopt an authoritarian demeanor. He resisted for a long time, but eventually, he did what I thought I wanted. One night, he rolled over in bed and told me he no longer found me attractive, that my fat thighs repulsed him. I was horrified; a real insult, as opposed to the orchestrated harshness I had daydreamed about, wasn't what I wanted from a lover, or a parent, or anyone. That night I told him to leave. Over the next year the sting of that cold remark convinced me that I didn't need to be hurt anymore to feel like a woman.

I went into treatment for depression and several years later met Christopher, my fiancé, who would praise the round of my thighs and the soft circle of my belly. I'd like to think I would have come to accept my womanly body without his approval, but I can't pretend it didn't help.

In the intervening years that have passed since my father's surgery I have had to reinvent the mythology of family. Liberating the notion of father from that of man hasn't been easy. I get wistful when I see cheesy Hallmark cards with dads tending the backyard barbecue or ads claiming that Father would like nothing more for his birthday than a lawn mower or a new tie. I still miss my dad, and there are times I sleep wearing his old gold Rolex. But my father is alive because she is female, and she has made herself into one hell of a woman. As she has grown into her womanhood, she has stopped the frenetic housecleaning and flower arranging. These days, she cooks only pasta, and several years ago she joined a women's bowling league, making her the Renee Richards of Ohio.

I still struggle now and then with the selfishness she exhibited during my childhood. I can get furious with her over the smallest disagreement. But for the most part, we spend less of our time arguing over whether she's a woman and more commiserating on how difficult it is to be one. She scolds me when I stew about having a bubble butt, and I console her when she gets dissed by a lesbian who can't deal with her male past. I still ache over the dissociation she felt with her own body and life. I comfort myself with recognizing that at least these days her struggle is ours together, and in the pact we have made, I found a father I never had.

ACTING LESSONS

Peter Snow

January. The last night of winter break. My parents are at it again in the kitchen. In the den, I sit cross-legged in front of our old TV, trying to focus on Stupid Pet Tricks.

I could tell there was going to be a problem as soon as my father came home with a big bouquet of irises for my mother. She isn't much for his romantic gestures. "You don't like them?" he asks. "I thought they were very nice. I thought you'd really like them."

"They're beautiful," she says, "but—"

"Then what's the problem?"

"You just . . . you shouldn't have. We're trying to save money right now." Water running.

"I thought I was doing something nice for you. I'm so stupid for thinking I could actually do something to make you happy." Cabinet slams shut.

"That's not the point," she hisses, "and I think Peter would like to hear his TV show, if you can keep it down."

For the next five minutes I hear the heated whispers firing back and forth behind me. I know the pattern. Their voices won't stay low for long. I flick off the television, no longer caring that there's a sheepdog peeling a banana on David Letterman's desk. It's time for me to go to bed.

I sneak past my parents in the dining room to the stairs. They both look at me out of the corner of their eyes as I go by, but the soft angry words never stop. Upstairs in my room, I shut the door and turn off the overhead light. I lie in my bed with a penlight and try to read a few chapters of Isaac Asimov, but I'm quickly distracted by my parents stomping up the stairs and past my room into theirs.

"I don't want to talk about it," my mother says.

"Well, I do," my father spits in response.

Their door clicks closed. I toss the book and the penlight on the floor. I curl the ends of the pillow up to cover my ears and try to think about school. I'll be back there tomorrow. I can still hear them through the pillow.

I look at the clock. Oh God. It's only 12:15. They fight for another few hours before I finally fall asleep.

FEBRUARY. CHOOSING AN ANNIVERSARY card is difficult, since it's supposed to be for both my parents, and in twenty-two years I have yet to find anything—from a personality trait to an interest—that they share. My mother doesn't go for understated greeting cards. Hallmark's patented rhyming verse tends to make her cry. Rainbows, little bears, and all manner of things sparkly are a plus. I'm not sure what kind of cards my father actually likes, but considering his inclination to reassemble engines as a hobby and spend hours in the basement building a fifth shelving unit for the bathroom, the cards I get him usually feature a cartoon dad wearing a tool belt and making a crack about "man's work."

I rifle through the measly selection at the 50-percent-off card store near campus and come across an anniversary card featuring wild horses running through a valley. "The love you share . . ." No good. That one goes back. Here's one that looks kind of like a velvet painting with a man in a tux and a woman in an evening gown sipping champagne in a ballroom. "Today we celebrate the romance . . ." Nope. I try a glossy card that plays "Moon River" when you open it. "Your love was meant to be . . ." Screw it. I get the one with the horses.

I wish I didn't have to buy them anything. But I guess if anyone's going to remind my parents of their wedding day, it should be me, the person who brought them there. If it weren't for little Pete-the-zygote popping up in my mother's womb, I honestly doubt she would have found herself, at the age of eighteen, standing before the justice of the peace with her boyfriend of two months, twelve dates, three makeout sessions, and four arguments. I still blanch when I think about what her mother— a resolute Irish Catholic who carries a plastic vial of Lourdes holy water in her pocketbook—or his mother—a resolute Italian Catholic who hangs wrought-iron crosses in every corner of her cluttered house—must have thought. Would that be fifteen Hail Marys? Thirty-seven Our Fathers?

But they must have been gratified when my parents did the honorable thing and entered into a loveless marriage—not to mention years of bickering and bitterness—to make sure that I got raised right. Had I the capacity to do so, I would have raised my objections right then from underneath my mother's graduation-cum-wedding gown.

I was never deluded into believing my parents were happy together. Even at four years old, I could hear the difference in the way my mom said, "I love you" to me and the halfhearted way she said it to my dad. And I'd wonder why my father would sit me down and tell me that my mother was the most important thing in my life, when an hour later he'd yell at her and reduce her to tears. But I know it would have been difficult for anyone in their situation.

Having never gone on to college or pursued jobs that paid comfortably above the poverty level, there was never much money coming in, and always differing opinions on how to spend what little there was. My mother stayed in the house all day with me, while my father worked a double shift lugging boxes at a warehouse, coming home to our one-bedroom apartment just in time to kiss me good night before he and mom started their usual argument. And by age seven or eight, I became saddled with the awareness that they lived in this state of perpetual misery for my benefit. It wasn't necessary. I would have been fine with the two of them deciding to call it quits. I'd see TV shows where kids were all broken up over their parents getting divorced, and I'd wonder what their problem was. When I was in high school, there was a period of a few months where my father was going out alone every weekend to "take a long walk in the park." He'd leave the house, and I'd wistfully ponder the idea of him having an affair. That would surely be enough to break up my parents' marriage. But, illicit lover in the park or no, my dad just eventually stopped going there, and nothing at all changed at home.

When I was fourteen, my mother started working at the corner grocery, and my father got a new job at a new warehouse. We were finally able to move into a real house, with more rooms and, thankfully, more places to hide. Both my parents acted as if we were about to enter a new golden age for our family. I was not fooled. Until I was able to scrounge up enough money to finance my own way into college, the years in that house just dragged on and on, with my only true moments of peace being when one parent or the other was gone. I couldn't wait to be off at school. Once I was gone, I figured, they would have nobody but themselves to blame for staying together.

MARCH 23RD. 3:22 P.M. My mother straightens the fruit-shaped magnets on the refrigerator for the third time in ten minutes as I sit at the kitchen table, my foot tapping nervously. Now that the plastic apples and pears are all stem up, I look up to hear the news she'd called me in to tell me. Her eyes sweep right past me and focus on a smattering of who-knows-how-old crumbs on the table. Letting out a long slow breath, she uses one hand to sweep the debris off the table into the upturned palm of her other hand. Her head darts back and forth, apparently in search of some place to deposit the crumbs. *Someone's dead*, I start to think as my mother stands with her back to me scraping at something on the countertop with a well-manicured fingernail. *Or maybe they're getting divorced.* I pick up a pen and start tapping it against the edge of the over-full ashtray between the salt and pepper pigs.

3:28 P.M. I'm worrying. This is just so typical of why I hate coming home. My dorm room back at school is a stark but peaceful haven for me; this house, on the other hand, is a constant source of torment. The moment I walked in the door, I found myself longing for the comfort of my borrowed bed.

Evil, wicked spring break! I'm stuck at home for two weeks knowing that one of my parents will inevitably snap at the other and trying to be prepared to duck out of the line of verbal fire when it happens. I'll have to pretend I somehow don't hear when the yelling starts—*this deodorant commercial on TV is just so fascinating, I can't hear a word you're saying*—and bolster my nerves of steel so I don't flinch when the door slams. Why did the stupid university have to force us home for the break? So they could fumigate? Damn the school. Damn the roaches. Damn the stupid bastard down the hall who always had a ham sandwich or a Pop-Tart lost under his desk or behind his bed. And damn my bank account for being too small to allow me to fly to Cancun with my friends, like people are supposed to do on spring break.

3:31 P.M. My fist slams down onto the table, but my brain doesn't register that fact until I notice the avalanche of cigarette butts I just started. I immediately yank a paper napkin out of the cracked plastic holder and begin to scoop up the butts.

"Sit," my mom says, "I'll get that." Great, I just gave her something else to clean.

"No, I got it," I say, jumping up. "So what's up?" I ask, trying to force eye contact.

"Okay," she says, very slowly and deliberately. "What would you think if I told you I was a lesbian?"

I sit back in my chair. A lesbian. My mother's a lesbian.

Goddamn it, I think, as my mother searches my face anxiously for some sort of response, how come I didn't figure this out earlier? That's what she was so afraid to tell me. Suddenly, upon hearing that one magic word, "lesbian," I understand why my parents' marriage has always been so shaky, why so much tension always existed between them, why it never seemed quite right to see them kiss, why my father's constant pushes for affection often snowballed into my mother's anger. Sure, they fight about money and the house and how to raise me and lots of other stuff, too, but I bet, if I try, I can draw it all back to this lesbian thing. Besides, I'm a theater major. Half of my friends are either gay or want to be. This is not bad. This is the best news I could have heard.

"Oh," I say. "That's fine."

"You're okay with this?" she asks incredulously.

"Yeah," I reply. "I guess I could've figured it out, actually." I always thought it was odd that a forty-year-old woman had so many sleepovers at her friend's house.

"Figured it out?" she asks, a look of pure terror replacing the wincing insecurity that had been on her face. "You can tell?"

"I mean, there are clues that kind of fit together if you know what you're looking for," I reply. My mother starts biting her overlong fingernails, and I look at her puffed-out mane of once-frosted hair and baggy sweatshirt with glittery kitten appliqué. "You don't, you know, look gay or anything. It's just that—"

"Because you can't tell anyone!" Her words slice like a guillotine blade. "This is my secret. Your father already knows, and I'm telling you now, but I'm not ready to deal with this yet with anybody else. Okay?"

I remain silent.

"Promise me," she repeats.

Now this is bad. This is awful. For a fleeting second, the revelation I'd just received seemed like the Rosetta Stone for understanding all of my family's problems, but now I have to pretend I never heard it.

I look into her pleading eyes.

This is just temporary. She needs some time to sort things out before making any public proclamations about her sexuality and the state of her marriage. I can accept that.

3:36 P.M. "Okay," I nod, biting my lower lip. I try to smile reassuringly. "I promise."

APRIL. I'M BACK AT school. Johanna, a good friend of mine, is deciding how to come out to her parents.

"It's just that my parents are so conservative, you know?" she says with an exhalation of cigarette smoke. "But we've always been close. And now, with Janis, I'm so happy, you know, and I feel like it's really lame that they don't know why, like it's this deep, dark secret or something."

"Mmm," I respond.

"I've tried to bring it up before, but they don't seem to want to hear it," she goes on. "Sometimes I think it would be best to just tell them, but I honestly don't know how they'd react. It could be awful."

I want to console her or give her advice, but I'm terrified to even broach the issue. What if I slip? What if Johanna just guesses from something I say?

"Yeah. That sucks," I say. Johanna leaves the room, and I bury my face in my pillow and cry. I sure as hell hope my mother appreciates this.

WHEN LOUIS HENRY THREW my Scooby-Doo lunch box in the Dumpster in third grade, I wasn't that upset, because I knew I could go home to my mother and she would shower me with hugs, kisses, and praise for her smartest, sweetest little boy in the universe. When Johnny Riley smashed baked beans into my hair, my mom perched crosslegged on my bed and pumped me up for two hours, explaining, as I sniffled into her lap, how much cooler I was that I didn't need to make other people feel small in order to feel important. My mother always made me feel worthwhile, no matter what kind of torment I went through at school. Every crayon still life and dried-macaroni sculpture I made was displayed with pride about the house. A kiss on the cheek rewarded every A or B. And in high school, when Doreen Blake told the other girls how ugly I was and Rich Falzone wrote the word *faggot* across the back of all my textbooks, my mother still assured me that I was intelligent, handsome, and very, very special. It didn't really work by that time, but I was grateful for the effort.

MAY. HOME AGAIN. I unlock the door, step inside, and drop my bags.

"Helllooo," my mother cries from the living room. She's sitting on the sofa with Jackie. Jackie is the slightly dowdy, pleasantly plump manager from my dad's first warehouse job. She cracks her gum a lot and always brings over videotapes of "The Nanny." She is my father's longtime friend and, as I've recently learned, my mother's lover. All three are sitting together on the couch—Dad, Mom, and Jackie—watching "Home Improvement." This doesn't seem healthy to me.

"Hi," I say, turn around, and walk right back out of the room.

"Hey," my dad calls. "We haven't seen you in months. Get back in here and say hello."

I turn around and slowly make my way over to the couch. "Hello, Dad. Hello, Mom. . . . Hey."

My mother stands up and envelops me in a powerful hug. "It's so good to see you," she says cheerily as I stare over her shoulder at my father and my mother's lover, both with grins plastered across their faces. They'd better be discussing who gets the house.

"Sit down," my dad says.

"How's school?" my mother asks, sitting back down between Jackie and my father.

I sit down in an armchair, as far as I can get from them, and flash a big, hopefully not too sarcastic, smile. "*School,*" I stress the word, "is great."

Don't get me wrong: I've got nothing against Jackie. If I came home to find her and my mom living together as a happy couple, Donna Reed and Harriet Nelson stirring up a fresh pot of Ovaltine, it would have been just dandy. If I'd found the two of them chugging Meisterbrau and screaming at the Packers game, that would have been OK, too. But this . . . I suddenly find myself praying to God to remove ménage-à-trois images from my mind.

"Classes: fine. Dorm: great. Friends: thumbs up." It's hard to form a complete sentence. Jackie's always been around. I've seen all three of them interact plenty of times before, but now, knowing what I know, I'm completely bewildered. Why isn't my dad blowing his top? Why is he so blasé about having his wife's lover in the living room? Why didn't he leave months ago? I would have.

I get up, fetch my bags, and take them up to my room. On the way, I'm told to hurry back down for dinner. At the dinner table, I watch my father passing Jackie the mashed potatoes. No way any of this would be happening if my mother had had an affair with a man.

Much to my relief, Jackie goes home for the night. I go to bed deeply confused. Everybody can't be copacetic with this arrangement. Then I hear the muffled angry voices rise from the other side of the bedroom wall. There is one word repeated so often that I am sure of what it is: "Jackie."

JULY. JASON, MY BEST friend, is on the way over to pick me up for a movie. He's known me and my parents since second grade. I haven't told him that my mother is a lesbian, even though she's still together with my father who shoots eight ball with my mother's lover who wants to take my mother away from him even though she's too scared to leave.

When he shows up, I rush him out of the house before he has a chance to engage my parents in small talk, and when he turns to me in the car and asks me how my mom is, I say, "Fine. Did you see 'The Simpsons' this week?"

AUGUST. MY MOM AND Jackie have gone off together for some quality time, leaving me alone in the house with my dad. He sits on the couch in his sweatsuit, eating Doritos and watching an old Chuck Norris movie. He can't be happy. His wife's in love with someone else. Does he think this is just a phase Mom is going through? Maybe it's pride. Maybe he's afraid of losing face if people find out. Maybe he doesn't think of a lesbian affair as a "real" infidelity, not as threatening as if she was doing the nasty with another man. Sometimes I wonder if he's clinging to the idea of being married, regardless of the reality. He needs someone to call "sweetie," someone to kiss when he gets home from work, and as long as he's got that he can tell himself he's content. He'll just pretend not to notice when she tenses up at his touch. I would give anything for him to have enough courage to move on.

I sit in the armchair next to the sofa. He turns to me.

"You gonna sit and watch a movie with your dad?" he asks.

"Yeah." I sit and watch the movie, silently.

DECEMBER. IN THE THEATER department dorm, everybody has his or her tragedy. Kneeling on the top bunk in her room, head bowed poignantly, Audrey tells the rest of us at the study session about the abortion she just had. After drinking a little too much at a party, football-player-turned-actor Jeff bursts into tears, going on about how he couldn't live up to his father's expectations for him to be a great athlete. Scott lets his Tater Tots burn in the community kitchen while he tells the others boiling their Ramen noodles that the true love of his life just slept with his best friend. Johanna sits smoking in the hallway, telling anyone who passes how she still hasn't owned up to her parents about her sexual orientation. All of them get doused with sympathy, encouraging words, and pats on the back.

At the end of the semester, right before winter break, a small group of friends is gathered in my room.

"I hate going home," I say. All heads turn to me. "My parents . . . my mom . . . it's just . . . it sucks, you know. I can't stand being there. My parents are just . . . they're just . . ."

"I know," says Jeff, "parents can be a pain in the ass."

"Yeah," Audrey throws in, "who wants to see their folks twenty-four seven?"

Johanna speaks up. "I've decided that, over the break, I'm definitely going to just come straight out and tell my parents. I'm going to spell it out for them plain and clear, and if they can't take it at first, I'll find a way for them to deal with it."

All attention turns to Johanna. I don't know if I'm annoyed or relieved.

CHRISTMAS HAS ME IN a haze. Random relatives mill about, passing gifts and quips back and forth all around me. I sit at the dessert table, eyeing my mother and father standing side by side, sipping their eggnog. I close my right eye, then my left, alternately blocking out one parent, then the other. That seems fine to me. Then I open both eyes and see them together like everybody else does. They're all being fooled.

My uncle approaches my father. "You get any lacy lingerie for the wife this year? Or is that her gift to you?" he jokes. My dad laughs along with him, my mother giggles nervously, and I shove a green-and-red-frosted cupcake into my mouth.

OVER THE WINTER VACATION, Jason confides in me that his brother is gay. I confide in him that my friend Johanna is gay.

JANUARY. "IS YOUR MOTHER okay? She doesn't look good." My grandmother asks this question. And I answer with the words that are beginning to become second nature: "I don't know."

I'm not giving her any false information, exactly.

"Looks like she might be sick." My grandmother pries further as she finishes washing the dishes and dries her hands on her sauce-stained apron. "Has she been sleeping?"

"I don't know," I try again. My grandmother pours me an un-asked-for Coke and slides a plate of homemade chocolate chip cookies toward me. She wants more. "I'm not in the house much these days," I say. "This is my only chance to see my friends, so I'm taking advantage of it."

"I worry about her," she goes on, wiping down the table with a wet rag. "I can tell there's something wrong with her. Maybe she should see a doctor. She's eating?"

"I'm sure," I answer. "I've been eating out a lot, though. I don't know."

"I hope she's okay," my grandmother says. "I can't help but worry."

"She's fine, Grandma."

Though the cookies smell delicious, my sudden butterflies stop me from trying one.

MARCH. I THINK TERRI really likes me. For the past few weeks, she's been stopping by my room a lot. She tends to sit very close to me, so our thighs are touching. She likes to lean over and whisper things in my ear that really don't need whispering, like "I think it's raining." When I ask her for a pretzel from the bag she's holding, she doesn't hand me one but instead holds one out so I have to eat it from her hand. She's very attractive, and it is so hard for me to keep telling myself this is all in my head.

APRIL. I HAVE A revelation. My mother is a lesbian. Though I've known this for a year, something hasn't truly sunk in until now. I'd always seen my mother hesitate just a little every time my father put his arms around her. She seemed to turn away or flinch from all of his kisses. A look of uneasiness would wash over her face every time he mentioned sex. She's a lesbian. A heterosexual woman probably wouldn't react that way.

That night I invite Terri to my room and lose my virginity.

MAY. I'VE HAD A few drinks, and for someone who's had about two full beers' worth of alcohol over his entire life span, that's enough to completely annihilate my inhibitions. "Where's my lesbian friend?" I repeat to myself like a mantra as I slalom through the dancing fools at the graduation party. I find Johanna and pull her out onto the back porch.

"What's wrong?" she asks with genuine concern.

"Isn't it cool out here," I say. "Look at the stars." It is, I think, the starriest sky I've ever seen.

"Yeah, it's beautiful," Johanna says. "You don't look so good. Do you need a ride home."

"No! Not home!" I explode, startling her. I take a deep breath, sit down on the porch steps, and reel myself in. "I just need to talk."

Johanna sits down next to me. "Well, talk. I'm listening."

"My mother's a lesbian," I blurt out so fast I'm not sure she understands it. But just to make sure she does, I reiterate, much more slowly. "My mother is a lesbian."

And then I can't stop talking.

I wake the next morning hungover with guilt. I'm rocking in my bed, thinking about all the years growing up, when my mother was my sole bastion against the hordes of classmates who teased me and made me feel inadequate. I call up my mom to tell her what a bastard I am.

She answers the phone and I blurt out, "I told Johanna last night. I had to tell someone, Mom. She's gay, too. I knew she wouldn't care. It was important, Mom. I had to. It helped. It was good for me. I had to. She's not going to tell anyone. I can trust her."

"All right," my mom says, trying to disguise the hesitance in her voice. "Okay. I understand you need someone to talk to."

"Yeah," I say. "Thanks."

"Jason doesn't know, though, right?"

"No. Jason doesn't know."

"Good. I'm not ready for Jason to know. We see him too much."

"Don't worry. He doesn't know." I hear my mother sigh with relief.

THREE YEARS LATER. I'M packing. I managed to find a roommate in New York. I'm going to be an actor. As my departure grows imminent, I am more excited than I can ever remember. The entire contents of my room have been squeezed into eleven cardboard boxes from the liquor store around the block, and now I run about the house gathering up anything else I claim as my own and tossing it all into a final shoebox. I grab a deck of cards from the coffee table, my favorite pen, the "World's Greatest Son" mug I've been drinking from since I was nine, and my framed college diploma.

"You're taking that?" my mother calls from the couch. She's lying there with a blanket pulled up to her chin, one arm curling out to tip a cup of hot tea to her lips. She's sick again. The same recurring worse-than-a-cold, less-severe-than-pneumonia illness that the Medicaid doctors can't diagnose. That they think might possibly be psychosomatic. That's been hitting her for the better part of a year since Jackie left town. I miss Jackie. Not that I knew her well myself, but I miss what she did for my mom. My mother practically glowed when she and Jackie were together. When Jackie left—moved away to another state by herself—I feared things would fall back to the way they were before. Instead, they got worse.

I put the diploma back up on the shelf. "I don't need it."

"You sure?" she asks. "If you really want it, take it."

My father walks in. "You almost ready?" he asks me. "You want help getting your stuff loaded on the U-Haul, we've got to do it now. I need to head back out to work in an hour."

"Give him a chance to say good-bye to his mother," Mom says, propping herself up against the sofa arm.

"All I'm saying is I haven't got all day," my father snaps back.

"He's moving out, for Christ's sake," she growls. "Why can't you just let him take his time?"

"I know he's moving out," he says. The words are sharp. "I still can't miss work."

"Isn't anything more important than your job?" she says.

"Oh, it's not important that I bring money into this house?" he says.

I lean down and give my mother a big hug. It shuts them both up. "I love you, Mom. I'll call you soon. Dad, I'll meet you outside." I grab a tequila box filled with old textbooks, and I head out the front door to the truck. I've made my decision. They'll make their own.

I REMEMBER REACHING FOR MICHAEL'S HAND

Stefan Lynch

Today I was waiting to pick up my lunch outside a restaurant in downtown San Francisco. There was a man my age sitting on the ground who (I found out later) was also waiting for his lunch. Suddenly, another man, whose eyes were bloodshot and clothes looked slept in, began to punch and kick the man on the ground, yelling at him as if he knew him, saying "Don't you ever mess with my shit again!" I stood frozen for a moment, then I began to yell at the punching man: "Stop it! Leave him alone!"

He kept kicking the man on the ground, who curled up in a ball, protecting his face. The attacker started to walk away, distracted, but then he turned around and took a running leap into the air and landed on the man on the ground, lost his balance, and fell down—dazed. Others joined in the yelling, and we got him to stop.

I knelt down to the man on the ground and sat with him while he cried. His hands were shaking when I gave him the piece of jewelry that had been knocked from his bleeding ear; he was hurt but not seriously. Then the police showed up.

They had the attacker in custody and wanted me to make a statement. The officer asked for my ID, my phone number, and my name, but I didn't want to tell him. I wouldn't have told him anything at all, but I wanted to show my support for the beaten man. My own hands began to shake as I handed the cop my driver's license and told him how to reach me. In the face of a violent assault, I was more frightened of the police than of the perpetrator.

My gay family never called the cops when I was growing up. The only assaults our friends reported to the police were assaults by the police. When my dad, a professor, was punched in the face by a former student screaming, "Faggot!" he did not report it. I was around thirteen at the time, and I definitely had the sense that, while it wasn't OK for this man to get away with beating up my dad, there was no recourse. The overall sense among my dad and his friends was that if you were gay, these things happened. Living in Toronto throughout middle school and high school, I was terrified of people finding out about my parents, partly because I might be rejected, but also because I dreaded violence. It's only since living mostly free of that fear that I have recognized its full impact. At the same time, the years I've spent living with my very-closeted mother have taught me that the shame of the closet is much worse than the openness of my dad's life, even if the act of being honest made us vulnerable to violence.

When I hid the truth about my family, I thought it was because I didn't want to be ostracized. I was a bit nerdy and awkward and out of place already without adding to it by outing my parents. But now I can more fully appreciate how my anxiety about the threat of antigay violence motivated my silence. I only caught a glimpse of that anxiety's true impact once or twice a year: usually at a Gay Pride march, when every step felt lighter, like a weight I didn't know was there had gone away. A friend's dad told her after he came out that "You have to be careful who you tell, there are people who would kill me if they knew." My dad never said those words, but he didn't have to: it was obvious.

I REMEMBER THE SUBWAY car pulling to a stop, the people inside swaying, and the people outside jockeying for position next to the doors. I remember reaching for Michael's hand—I always called both my parents by their first names—as we got off the train. I didn't want to be separated from him, although I took the subway downtown every school day by myself. Usually there was a crush of men and women in suits hurrying to bank jobs on Bay Street or law offices on Front, but this was the middle of the afternoon, an unusual time to be arriving, unusual people going about their business: shift-working West Indian women in their blue uniforms and practical shoes, young couriers with enormous bright bags covered with logos, drunks who rode the same train around and around in sleepy laps across Toronto.

On my dad's other side he carried his bag, a leather satchel that looked enough like a purse that I was sometimes embarrassed by it even though my parents had told me it was OK. Unlike my mother's purse, which was filled with tissues, tiny folding scissors in silk pouches, yogurt-covered peanuts, and loose change, Michael's satchel only ever held the material of the moment: fresh cheese, green beans, and European sausages bought from vendors in Kensington Market; essays graded in green pen to return to his students.

I remember climbing the stairs to the street slowly so that the other riders would pass. We stopped and my dad let go of my hand, reached into his satchel, pulled off the rubber band that kept the stacks of rectangular white stickers neatly in order, brought one out, peeled off its backing, and—with a focus that I think was determination not to look behind him—stuck the red-on-white decal at eye level on the green tile wall. It read in bold capitals:

NO MORE SHIT!
GAYS BASH BACK!

The image of it, stuck there for anyone to see, still burns in my mind's eye. I didn't understand all that was going on, but I did know that we were in the middle of some kind of fight, that my dad was gone most evenings until very late, that the phone was constantly ringing as I carefully wrote down the messages from lawyers and reporters and friends as my dad had taught me to do; they kept wanting me to read back what they had said. Remembering these things, I wanted to know more.

Michael, my father, is dead now, so I e-mail Rick, a friend of his with an encyclopedic memory who lived through those times in Toronto. I ask him to help me reconstruct a brief history of that time when, with my dad, he was part of the collective that ran the gay newspaper called the *Body Politic*. He tells me about the website of the Canadian Lesbian and Gay Archives, where he and others have posted timelines and essays about this period. It makes me feel old to have lived through something now considered history.

AT THE END OF 1977, when I was nearly six, Toronto police raided the *Body Politic* office, seizing financial records, subscription lists, unopened mail, and all copies of *The Joy of Gay Sex, The Joy of Lesbian Sex*, and *Loving Man*, books on hand for their mail-order business. The paper was charged with publishing obscenity. The next month, antigay crusader and former Miss America, Anita Bryant, had a campaign stop in town, and thousands protested. (Thanks to Ms. Bryant's campaign, I wasn't allowed to have orange juice at home; Bryant was the spokesperson for the Florida Citrus Growers.) Throughout the next year, the trial of the *Body Politic* moved forward; then, the Toronto police raided a gay bathhouse, as news came from San Francisco: the city's mayor, George Moscone, and gay politician Harvey Milk was dead, gunned down by Dan White, a homophobic former police officer turned politician.

I ask Rick about a picture I have of Michael from this time: it's taken from below so he looms in the sky with a big grin, holding a feather in one raised hand and a bullhorn in the other. Rick says that my dad is telling the crowd at a rally that they have a right to their pleasure.

After a fierce trial—I remember trying to sit still in the gallery one afternoon while a nervous police officer testified—the *Body Politic* was acquitted. *Now I'll see him more*, I thought. In May, Dan White succeeded with his "Twinkie Defense" in the San Francisco murders—lawyers argued he was stressed-out from eating junk food. On our fridge, next to the postcard of the Sisters of Perpetual Indulgence (an order of charitable drag queens) roller-skating down a San Francisco hill, was a newspaper clipping of "White Night," when gays, shocked and enraged by the judgment, rebelled and burned police cars throughout the city.

In February 1981, I had just turned nine when the Toronto police again raided gay bathhouses and arrested 280 men. The next night, three thousand people demonstrate in the streets in defiance of the police crackdown, and two weeks later, after dozens of activists postered the city with crack-and-peel stickers, even greater numbers came out in protest. Rick, I learn, designed those vibrant, red-and-white "No More Shit" stickers; he's still proud of their impact.

ALTHOUGH MANY OF THE striking events of my childhood related to my dad's gay activism, he tried hard to keep me out of the middle of things, out of harm's way. So I often saw the aftermath, like when he came home with a swollen face after being beaten by a former student, and I would have to pry to find out what had happened.

After dinner one night—a week after I came back from spending Christmas vacation with my mom and her partner, Pat—my dad, his lover Bill, and a friend of theirs from the university were talking. I was bored. Why, I wondered, if people came over for *dinner*, did they always spend so much time talking after dessert was long gone? It was too soon to excuse myself to play computer games, so I sat staring down at people's shoes through the glass tabletop. For the first time I noticed that one corner of the glass had an irregular, sharp scar-shaped chip. Pointing at it, I asked, "Michael, what happened?"

They were suddenly quiet. The guest from the university looked down at his hands, and my dad took in a breath.

"A brick," he said. "Someone threw a brick."

"Oh." I was embarrassed by my own question. It made everybody uncomfortable. "Nobody was hurt," added my dad, quickly. I learned later, when the guest had gone and the dishes were being washed, that the house had been empty when the brick shattered the double-paned glass of the front window, chipped the corner of the dining room table, scratched some paint off the wall, and came to rest on the gray carpet by the stairs leading up to the kitchen. A neighbor had seen two men, university age, running down the street some time that day. Had they thrown it?

Michael came home after teaching a class, dropped his books on the stairs to his study, and went into the kitchen to unpack the groceries from his satchel. When he turned around to put the milk in the fridge, he saw the gaping hole in the window and the scattered glass. His first thought was that a bird had crashed into it. He looked around for a carcass, stepping right over the brick as he came down the steps. It wasn't until he was crouching down to pick up the large pieces of glass with yellow rubber kitchen gloves and putting them into a cardboard box that he saw it lying in the corner by the steps, rusty-brown and still.

Memories of my childhood are sometimes vague, and like all memories, when details are sketchy, imagination fills them in. I can no longer tell the difference between what I actually was told and what details my own mind has provided. I'm not sure when the incident was or if the neighbor really did see people running from the scene. I wasn't around when it happened.

The story of the brick was one that my dad was uncomfortable telling; the student on the street directed his anger at my dad, but the brick was a more general attack against our home, and it therefore endangered me. My dad's self-conscious silence fueled my imagination. For instance, I never saw the brick, but I was told what was written on it. From this brief description I have constructed a sharp, brutal image in my mind's eye of thick white brushstrokes on the brick's red surface:

FAG.

Not having been there, not having seen the actual brick that my dad threw away, the only hard evidence I have that any of this happened is the chip in the table, which I now own. Maybe someone dropped a serving dish on that spot and there never really was a brick and I made it all up. It's a shaky memory, perhaps because my dad was so ashamed of bringing that danger into my world that I tried to forget it to help him save face.

A few years later, we feared we were being attacked again. When a yellow spray-paint stencil of a gavel appeared on our sidewalk, we thought that we were being targeted again: "Judgment," that gavel seemed to say. My dad told me to stay inside, and he left to find out more. When he came back, he hustled me off to school, but before I left I asked what he thought it was. He didn't know, he told me, but identical gavels were stenciled in front of all the houses of his gay friends.

I spent a nervous day at school. It wasn't a burning cross on the lawn, but it felt close enough.

When I got home, instead of finding my house bombed or my dad shot dead on the floor, I opened the door and heard laughing into the phone. "It's for the gay law conference at the university," he was telling someone. "They marked where the presenters live so the people from out of town will feel more at home."

NONE OF THIS HAD been part of the plan for my dad's life. Unlike many young college-educated men of his generation, my dad was too square and too green—not long off the bus from the rural South—to be in the middle of the anti–Vietnam War protests. He was not a sixties radical.

He and my mom are gawky in their wedding pictures, my dad with an awkward smile, messy red hair, and thick black-rimmed glasses, my mom looking shell-shocked and impossibly young. The pictures don't show my mom below the waist because my grandmother was aghast at the white miniskirt she wore and wouldn't allow anyone to photograph it. Except for the blood relatives, everyone is trying terribly hard to look hip—not easy in the middle of Iowa. A couple years later, pregnant with me, they moved to Toronto, on the other side of the border, so my dad could take a teaching job at the university.

My own memories of that border are far from the excitement they must have felt on that first crossing. Throughout my life, we could not carry anything clearly gay into the States—not a book or a button or a pink triangle. At first this was from a general fear of harassment or that such items might trigger a thorough search on suspicion of importing obscenity. Later it became a fear of rejection at the border after the United States made entry into the country illegal for HIV-positive people. My dad had theories on how to deal with the customs and immigration agents. "Always say you've been gone at least a week, or they will think you are smuggling cigarettes," he would tell me. "Don't look them in the eye for too long or they think you are lying." And, "Always go for a man. The women have to prove themselves."

Despite myself, I still go to the male agents.

READING RICK'S ESSAYS AND thinking critically about my dad, in a way that I can do only now that I'm an adult, helps clarify what happened that day on the streets of Toronto, after we had climbed the stairs from the subway station. It was the one time Michael brought me directly into danger. It was the one time the constant antigay threats and attacks happened with me present in a way that he could not conceal, or make light of, or smooth over.

There was a man in a gray coat and blue jeans following us. Had he come from the subway station like we did? He would stop at a bus shelter or telephone pole where Michael and I had just been. I couldn't tell what he was doing. My dad saw him, too, and started to work more quickly, peeling off the next sticker while we were walking, slapping it on the street sign or the phone booth and running his hands over it to make it stick, then moving on almost without stopping. We could do a couple a minute this way. I was in charge of stuffing the wax paper backing into my pockets when my dad handed it to me; you don't litter in Toronto.

I started losing sight of the man in the gray coat as we rounded corners, looking for surfaces, dodging scurrying pedestrians. Then we turned onto an alleyway that was a shortcut we took in the evenings from the YMCA to Dudes, the gay bar where I would play pinball while my dad ate clam chowder and flirted with friends. We were near the next block, where the dark alley opened up onto sunny Wellesley Street, when the man in the gray coat, red-faced and breathing hard, stepped in front of us.

Michael stopped dead and edged in front of me. I could see now that the man was wiry, and around my dad's age. He had a reddish beard, which needed to be trimmed, and small blue eyes, and he was shaking. He didn't block our path. Instead he stood in front of us to one side, a body's length away. My dad was not a big man, but he worked out because he was vain and the YMCA was the unofficial gay male community center and pickup joint. I doubt he had ever punched anyone in his life, but I hoped the man in the gray coat couldn't tell that.

I remember reaching for Michael's hand. Into the nervous silence he said to the man, "I'm going to keep walking."

"Stop putting up your fucking faggot stickers," said the man in the gray coat before my dad had finished. He spat the words, his voice shaky with tension. He looked poised to do something, his hands balled tightly.

My dad said in a steady, quiet voice, "I am going to keep putting them up. You can keep taking them down." Each word was measured. It was the same voice he used when he discovered the pieces of a favorite plate I had broken and hidden in the garbage, the whisper that made me cringe three rooms away. The man in the gray coat took a step forward, still staying out of arm's reach. I remember that he never looked at me even though I couldn't take my eyes off him.

This was the face of the bogeyman. Forever after, when I hear about someone being threatened or gay-bashed or murdered, it is the man in the gray coat that I imagine.

"I am going to keep walking," Michael said again, and he slowly stepped out onto the street, pulling me tightly after him.

MY MOTHER AND THE NUN

Kelley Conway

My mother was thirty-seven when she fell in love with a woman, the same age I am now. It was 1974, I was fourteen,
and the woman my mother fell in love with was the principal
of my brothers' and sisters' new grade school, a nun who belonged to the rather modern order of Saint Francis and who
also happened to be her boss.

As if this wasn't complicated enough, I had become infatu-
ated with one of my friends, a sloe-eyed Italian girl, with olive
skin and wide hips—a girl whose body felt soft whenever I
found an excuse to hug her.

THE NIGHT THAT COMES back to me from that year is a Friday. The family has eaten dinner, Sister Joyce is over, and I
want to attend a basketball game at my high school. So the
three of us—Joyce, my mother, and I—get into the station
wagon. I sit in the backseat and stare out the window, spacing
out like a good adolescent, answering only the questions they
address directly to me, which are not many. They are absorbed
in each other. My mother's hair has been cut short, and though
her face is a perfect oval, feminine and pretty, her predilection
for long shirtwaists and tailored clothes, combined with the new
hair, conspire to make her look like a nun. Later, I will discover
that lesbian couples have this tendency to blur styles and resem-
ble each other, but at fourteen, as we turn toward the convent
to drop Joyce off and I look at my mother's short, frosted hair,

I don't think of this at all. I think, *Get it over with, will you? I don't want to be late.*

We pull into the driveway of the convent, and Sister Joyce says a short good-bye to me, a long one to my mother. The car is dark, only the lights of the dash shining dimly upward, toward their faces. When Joyce bends toward my mother, her short veil falls forward, but not enough to obscure my view. Without shame, she kisses my mother on the lips. I watch their lips like simple physical objects. I see them press together, smooth out; I see my mother look into Sister Joyce's eyes. And in that one moment the world changes. The skin on my body begins to tingle; I can feel each separate pore. And I am frozen. When Joyce gets out of the car I can't move, not even to get in the front seat with my mother. She has to tell me three or four times before I get out of the car, slam the door, and place myself on the vinyl seat as far away from her as possible.

I sit there, my thoughts moving so fast they blur into nothing. My body is still tingling, but my legs seem unattached. I must order them to cross and uncross. My mother is a lesbian, and I have had exactly three months in an all-girl high school, three months free of mockery, free of boys, and maybe that is all I will ever have. Because I am a lesbian, too, and I don't want to be, I don't want to be like my mother, I don't want to be made fun of, I don't want to be different, and I am—not just smarter, or too needy, or too scared to punch one of those stupid boys.

I may be mocked for the rest of my life.

I may be just like the mother who has never defended me against my father's violence; who tells me I'm pretty, but when she thinks I don't notice, scrutinizes me as if she's trying to understand what's wrong with me; who is cold and feminine and tense and just now beginning to soften.

I say good-bye to my mother when I get out of the car, and then I slam the door as hard as I can.

The lights inside the school gym are bright, a shock after the dim underwater glow of the car. Cheers, screams, and noise, lots of it. A group of girls call to me, and though I climb through the stands feeling welcomed, I am also floating through the lights and the noise, up to the vaulted ceiling, and I have to watch the other girls to know when to stand or cheer. Mostly, I'm quiet, and my mind is occupied by the image of lips meeting. I think that I have never seen my parents kiss, and when my father reaches out to hug my mother or pinch her or tease her, she frowns and moves out of reach. Just as I do.

In the middle of this, one of my friends grabs my shoulders from behind and, in the excitement of the game, hugs me. I have never been so tense. I think the girl is a lesbian, like my mother, like Joyce, and she had better leave me alone or I will deck her.

The next week, at school, I avoid this girl. I can barely say hello. I can't call her, can't talk, won't make plans, and though I know, even at fourteen, that this is cruel, I can't stop myself. I want to. I am not a mean person. But I think if that girl touches me again I will die.

It takes me three years to apologize to her, and when I do, I still can't explain.

FOR THE REST OF that year, I stayed close to Maureen Bryson, my best friend, whom I was gratefully not attracted to, whom I could hug in safety, both of us in our polyester green uniforms and identical short haircuts over turned-up noses and freckles, though I was some eight inches taller than she was. We were both full of excitement that we had found a friend, and one we liked so much.

I told Maureen everything—everything except that my mother was a lesbian, everything except that I might be one, too. It never occurred to me to tell. Though the high school we attended was twenty minutes away by car, though I had left the boys of grade school behind, their voices still echoed in the moments before I fell into sleep in my narrow twin bed: barking, name-calling, laughing as they hung notes on my back, as they created circles on the playground and trapped me inside them.

THE CLOSEST MY MOTHER and I ever came to talking about her relationship with Joyce back then was during a fight. Even when I walked in on them kissing on the king-sized bed in my parents' bedroom, even after Sister Joyce had taken up residence in that bed most weekends and my father had started sleeping in the den, we didn't talk. But during this one fight—I was seventeen by then and dating boys to prove I wasn't who I already knew I was—I yelled at my mother, "At least I'm not a fucking lezzie!" I remember the shocked vulnerability on my mother's face. I remember it because our fights were endless by then, and she never gave in. Neither did I. But when I said that, she stopped fighting, she told me we needed to talk, and suddenly she could say nothing. What could she say?

I wanted to know if they got genital. I told myself that was all I needed to know, that I was not watching my mother's blue eyes and her steady matronly body for clues to a world safe for women who loved each other.

My mother worked for Sister Joyce five days a week, and of course, she did more than her job. With typical efficiency, she made Joyce's life easier in every way she knew how. Did I recognize the stages of partnership in a relationship so different from my parents' long battle for power? Sister Joyce and my mother spent time together after work and on weekends, whenever they could. They developed a daily life, composed of work, then afternoon cocktails they drank sitting next to each other on the couch, so close the entire length of their legs touched. Joyce smiled at my mother with love, and my mother, always shy, sat in the warmth of that smile like a loved child who knows she will be cherished, who knows she has been found.

I think my mother loved Joyce immediately—not without reservation, because that was not her way, but with a sense of miraculous discovery. I think my mother discovered happiness; she had never found it before.

Still, even with Joyce in her life, my mother remained pinned to my father, afraid she could not give herself or her six children the home, the vacations, the comfort that he provided. A closed woman of German descent, she told me nothing. If I looked to her for answers, silence was the most consistent one I found.

ONCE MY MOTHER TOLD me that she didn't like to talk the way I did. I had been telling her about an experiential psychology class I'd taken in college, one in which we'd turned pillows into our parents. I had screamed at the one with her name, begging it to see me.

"And you like that?" she asked. "You actually want to do things like that?" She shook her head with her mouth drawn to one side, and I knew she was thinking she would never understand me. "I just don't like to analyze everything like you do," she told me. "I don't like all these deep conversations."

I hated her for saying it, and more for it being true, but I was also grateful. It was an honest thing to say, and it let me know that I was alone in my searching—that she could not, and never would, help me.

TEN YEARS AFTER MY mother first fell in love with Joyce, I came home from Europe with hairy legs. I was twenty-four and had already had my first serious relationship with a woman; my mother had finally left my father, but Joyce had been transferred to another convent because of rumors about their relationship, which was already starting to wane.

Of course, I had told my father and the older siblings that I was bisexual (what I then called myself) four or five years earlier, but I hadn't told my mother. She found out by reading letters I sent to one of my sisters.

One night, when we were alone in her townhouse, sitting on the couch, she reached over and tugged at the hairs on my legs.

"So you're bisexual, eh?" she said. Then she gave me one of her shy smiles.

I was the one who didn't know what to say. "Maybe I am," I finally answered.

"I know."

There was a strange silence.

"Well, what about you and Sister Joyce?" I asked.

"We were soul mates," my mother said. "I've never had a friend like that before."

It was the most she had ever said, the most she ever would say.

Now she is married to a man, and last June I married a woman. I am the same age my mother was when she fell in love with Joyce. She did not attend my wedding, but I was thinking of her, and the ways that I have always completed her life. I thought of the answers I wanted as an unpopular fourteen-year-old girl, answers she couldn't give me, and I wondered whether love or writing or even activism has helped me to become a woman who is less her daughter. Sometimes, in this vast intolerant world of ours, I think I am still sitting in the backseat of that station wagon watching a kiss, knowing what it will mean for the rest of my life; and I am afraid. Then I remember the softening of my mother's face, and I know that my marriage is the farthest thing from silence. Last June, I bent into a kiss of my own. It was my choice, and it is my answer.

MORAL FABRICS*

Jennifer DiMarco

These are the first things I learn.
I am a round, warm, bald-headed baby. Pale skin, giant eyes. Blue eyes like great-grandma Nanna, who was the first in my family to come to America. Small head like a cue ball. Four pounds at birth. I am the first grandchild on either side.

They call me Number One, Big Eyes, Owl Head, and a thousand renditions of Darling, in three different languages.

I am born into a world of pasta, potato pancakes, red wine, and honeyed ham. I am borne into the world by my mother, who gave up everything and married in black just to have me. She writes children's stories instead of novels.

My father helped, too, I suppose. He gave up nothing, except his life.

FLANNEL

Him. Father.
I sit on a still lap. I am two. He is silent. He. I know that. He is not Mama. I never learn to say Daddy. I have one hand in his long hair. He is smiling, but it's hard to tell what's real. Sometimes people smile and pretend they're happy when they want to cry. I know that, too. No one told me. I found out myself.

I sit on one knee; a musty cigar box full of bullets sits on the other. The bullets are cold and slick. There are so many of them. I reach out and wrap a tiny hand around a 158-grain hollow point. My fingers just reach around it. He looks at my hand. He looks at me. He isn't smiling. His tears are the first I ever see.

HIS LONG HAIR COVERS his soft face. He is crying in Mama's arms. He's shaking, he's so scared. I am scared. We live in a one-room apartment, the floors and walls bare, the refrigerator empty. Mama has two jobs, and he is too frightened to work, even to leave the house. I know what all this means. Because the rest of the world must never find out this secret: his fear, Mama's strength. I have to be perfect so no one sees the rest.

IT'S BETTER TO HAVE *a gun and not need one than to need one and not have one.* These are the words scrawled on the back of our door. I can read them, but I don't know what they mean. He wrote them. He also drew the gun beside them. I know what guns are.

MAMA IS AT HER night job. I am in a fourth-hand high chair. He should be cooking dinner. The smell of grease and chicken waft from the minuscule kitchen. But there is also a new odor in the apartment. Sour, sharp, strong. It comes from him, asleep on the couch, and the spilled bottle that has soaked his flannel shirt, one cuff dripping onto the floor.

When he sleeps he is not afraid, and so I am silent. I am a good baby. Then there comes another smell, quickly overwhelming the others. I remember it as a thick black smoke. Then the smoke parts like an opening mouth and I scream, because there is fire behind it.

Mama saved us from that fire. She picked me up, high chair and all, and went back in to drag him out as well. I sat outside in my chair, watching my world drown in liquid fire while Mama pulled him out, the flames melting the flesh off her hands.

That is the last memory I have of him. Asleep there, on the

couch, his flannel shirt dripping alcohol. I do not remember him ever talking to me. I cannot place his voice or gestures. He was like a little boy, though; I think I knew that even then.

Mama and I moved away. I never saw him again. No one saw him. Angel, my baby sister, was born. She never knew our father. His parents told me he had gone on a long business trip. They showed me where he had gone on their big map. I was four, almost five, and I knew they were lying.

I did not miss him until I was nineteen.

Mama's parents told me he had something wrong with him. He was too scared, and it got him in trouble.

The FBI told me to go to my room.

Mama told me the truth ten years later. That day I learned that no one knows where he went. No one knows where you go when someone kills you.

Perhaps that young man with the long brown hair and the eyes full of tears was right all along. Perhaps my father should have been afraid.

DENIM

Her. Mama.

Mama has black curly hair with wisps of auburn and pale brown. She has blue eyes like mine and Nanna's. She has olive skin like Angel's. She is twenty years old when I am born. Twenty-four when Angel is born. She lives for us, and we adore her.

Mama is always smiling a brave, tough smile. She has only one rule: don't lie to me. We never do. She works double jobs, but somehow she's always there to drive us to school in the morning and tuck us in at night. We don't know where she works, but she sells something to someone. She makes something. She makes do.

Mama knows everything. She can do anything. She can answer any question and build things and lift things. She can also be quiet and read to us or just sit and hold us when we have nothing to eat.

Mama dresses in sweaters or T-shirts and coveralls, boots

that have hard toes, and worn denim jackets. She doesn't care if what she wears matches or if it's old. We dress like her. We're clean children, but our hair is scraggly, tangled and uncut for years. We don't know what "school shopping" is or what it's like to have a man in the house. We know phrases like *food bank, work for it*, and *slum lord*.

I sit in the circle of her arms. She is the best mama in the world. She can do no wrong.

I have nightmares, and she makes a special pillow that will take them away. She reads me a story about how love is strength and shows me her byline. She pulls a quarter from behind my ear and an egg out of a hat.

She is magic.

WE ARE OUT WALKING. We have to go to the store, but the motorcycle is broken. The sky is dark with no moon. We buy eggs. Mama holds Angel on her shoulder, and I hold Mama's hand.

Her hand is the strongest in the world. It is warm and smooth. I hold it tighter. When I grow up, I think, I want to have Mama's hands.

A man steps out from behind a willow tree. I jump. He calls my Mama a name I have never heard before. He calls her *dyke*.

She is very still and she says something back, "Wha'z it ta you, prick?" Her New York accent shows, and I can tell what's going to happen. She is still because she is ready. The man says *dyke* again, and he comes forward. Mama hands me Angel and stops the man from coming any closer.

We leave him there on the sidewalk. I don't pay attention to his moans because I don't care. Mama takes Angel again. She had never let go of the eggs; none of them are broken.

I LEARNED TO TELL time. I learned to make tea. At 6:00 A.M. I would slip off the mattress Angel and I shared and kiss her on the head. I would boil water. In my long T-shirt I would stand by the front door. The bare floor was always cold. At 6:30

Mama would come home. Her eyes would almost be shut. She was exhausted. It hurt me to see her so tired. She was not smiling. I would take her coat, help her off with her boots, and bring her tea. I was almost six. She needed me.

But somehow, one early morning as I walked back to the mattress, I knew Mama needed more. She needed someone else. Mama needed a partner.

SILK

Her. Mumu.

The first thing I know about the woman who will become my mumu is her perfume. The scent to me means nobility and luxury and the exotic. Before her, I had never known anyone who wore perfume. Everyone I know smells like hair and skin and clothes. But this new scent of dancing spices and flowers lingers in every room. It's strongest in the corner of the living room where Mama's mattress is. Strongest when Angel and I come home after being gone at school all day.

Other changes begin to happen. The house is cleaner. There are new cups and bowls. A bright green plant appears in the hall. New toothbrushes. And food. Cereal and oatmeal and fruit and bread and just-for-kids vitamins find their way into our big open cupboard. I hold Angel up so she can see in, and her eyes are as big as the navel oranges.

Then Mama tells us she has fallen in love with a woman. She has found us Mumu. A certain kind of joy seeps through me. I hug Mama tightly. Her happiness makes my world shine.

MUMU HAS GINGER HAIR and green eyes. Her face is softer than Mama's, but her body has the same small toughness. She wears simple glasses. She works at a large company and takes classes to become a therapist. She drives a car, not a motorcycle. She works in her garden with gloves over her hands and clean oval nails. She wears slacks and silk blouses, all in bright colors. She is not the same kind of woman Mama is—she does not fix cars, swear at injustice, or fight with strangers four or five times a week. She meditates, she frowns, she talks about human behavior.

Mumu is the type of woman who does not hesitate to fall in love with a twenty-six-year-old widow and her two young children who live on the receiving end of poverty. Mumu is strong.

Mumu smiles at us. She takes out her keys and opens her front door. Angel and I walk into the house holding hands. Our mouths are agape in amazement. Mumu has a fireplace. She has a washing machine, a dryer, a toilet that doesn't leak, a bathtub without cracks. Mumu has carpets, curtains, cupboards full of rice and cereal and soup and glass jars packed with pasta.

She shows us a staircase. The house has two floors! We climb the steps and she shows us two rooms, two beds, two dressers, two desks, two toy chests. One room has wood paneling and a shelf full of books. The other room is painted pink and white and has a pillowed window seat. Angel stares up at Mumu. "Would you like to come live here with me?" Mumu asks.

Angel nods vigorously, then looks to me for approval. I meet Mumu's gaze. "Can Mama come, too?" I ask.

ONCE A MONTH MUMU cooks a Thanksgiving dinner. The turkey is always so big that Mama helps me carry it to the table. Angel carries the cranberry sauce or the mashed potatoes or the peas. We gather together and Mumu says a prayer: Dear Goddess, thank you for bringing us together, for letting us find each other in the world. Thank you for making us a family.

Mumu has many rules, not just one like Mama, but we don't mind. Her rules are good rules. No drugs. No alcohol. No guns.

Mumu tells us that if someone breaks into the house, we should just be quiet and let them take anything. Things can be replaced. And even your own gun can be used against you.

I think of him. I know Mumu is right.

Our family is complete. I love my parents with all that I am. I would die for them. I will live for them.

SKIN

Time passes. My parents are my balance; Angel is my friend to laugh with, my little sister to protect, and my co-conspirator against the part of the world that is against our mothers. We learn so early that difference is feared and hated.

We survive ridicule, rock throwing, and rumbles. We survive job losses, car wrecks, and revisiting the food bank.

Angel survives being behind the other students at school because of the poor education offered to us before Mumu came. Angel graduates as her class's valedictorian.

I survive being kidnapped and raped. I survive to escape and to write about being a survivor. It works. I do a dozen interviews on the radio and in the papers. I am dubbed a "whiz kid," a "prodigy."

Four months after I turn eighteen, I leave home for the first time to embark on a book tour. I am prepared. Mama gave me her fists. Mumu gave me her voice.

---

*This essay is excerpted from a longer piece that originally appeared in *Generation Q*, edited by Robin Bernstein and Seth Clark Silberman (Alyson Publications).

FREAK

Morgan Green, with Ellen Samuels

H ow do they do a sex-change operation?"
My cousin Ann rolls over and stares down at me on my makeshift bed of couch cushions and sheets on the floor. We are sleeping over at our grandparents' house, and I have been waiting all week to ask her this question. Ann is eight, so she knows things.

"Well," she answers slowly, "they find a man and a woman who both want to be the opposite sex. Then the doctor takes off the male parts and puts them on the woman, and takes off the female parts and puts them on the man." Satisfied, Ann nods her head and rolls back toward the wall.

In a few minutes, I can hear her breath slowing down, as she falls asleep. But I am still wide awake—and scared to death. When Mom and Jamie sat me down a few days ago and told me about the operation that Jamie was going to have, I didn't remember them saying anything this horrible. In fact, I barely remember what they said at all. I think I forgot their words just as soon as I heard them. But now, in light of Ann's new information, I really can't understand why Jamie would want to go through such an awful operation. I think about last week, when Jamie came home from work at 7:00—early enough to tuck me in. I rushed into my room and got under the covers as quickly as possible while Jamie set down her briefcase and made her way to my room. She sat down on my bed in her formal gray jacket, and began what we like to call "the did today ceremony," where we tell each other everything we did that day. She didn't say anything about switching parts then, either.

I wonder if things will be the same after Jamie has the operation. I wonder if it will hurt. Most of all, I wonder what man Jamie will be trading parts with. Why, I puzzle, do people want to have other peoples' bodies, anyway?

NOW THAT I AM, at age fifteen, way more knowledgeable than most grownups about this whole sex-change thing, Ann and I can giggle over that childhood conversation about Jamie, who I now call my dad. "I didn't know what I was talking about," she tells me. "I was really scared and confused about the whole sex-change thing. The first time I saw your dad after he started taking hormones, I actually ran and hid. He looked so different with a beard and a flat chest."

"I was scared, too," I tell her. I was only three at the time, too young to remember much—just little snippets, like that late-night question-and-answer session with my cousin. The only moment when Dad stopped being a woman that I remember clearly is when he had the surgery to get rid of his breasts and had thick white bandages wrapped around his chest for weeks. I can also vaguely recall him lying on the couch in his pajamas, recovering from one of his operations for something or other. I was entranced by the container that the hospital had given him to vomit in. It was bright pink (my favorite color at the time), shaped like a large kidney bean with measurements in ounces up the side. I thought it was beautiful, even though I knew it wasn't supposed to be.

WHEN I WAS IN fourth grade, I transferred to a new school where no one knew about my parents' past. The first people I ever actually told about Jamie were my best friends in fifth grade, Lauren and Briana. Lauren was Iranian, tiny with olive skin and wavy dark hair. We had a passion for writing, though she also wanted to be a doctor. Briana had long blond hair and brown eyes and was the nicest person I'd ever met. Unlike Lauren or other kids I knew, Briana was seldom self-absorbed and was almost always considerate of other people's feelings. I felt protected by her.

I had felt just awful about keeping my mom's lesbianism and Jamie's transsexualism such a big secret, when friends were supposed to tell each other everything, no matter what. So, one rainy Friday afternoon in the after-school day-care room, I told Lauren and Briana about my mom being a lesbian. They weren't too surprised. They had already figured that one out, after seeing my mom's girlfriend Siobhan, with her men's clothes and dark, short hair. But I really startled them with my next revelation.

"My father was a woman," I said in what I hoped was a calm, matter-of-fact voice.

Lauren just nodded, her eyes wide as she murmured, "Whoa . . . that's really weird, Morgan. But okay, I guess. No big deal."

But Briana stared at me, open-mouthed. "Nuh-uh! You're so lying," she accused.

"I am not!" I didn't know how to convince her, so the next day I brought a picture of Jamie-as-a-girl to school. At recess, I motioned to Briana to come into the girls' room where I showed her the picture. In the photo, Jamie so closely resembles James, my dad, that's it's clear they're the same person, but she is also obviously a woman, with a female figure and smooth complexion instead of my dad's beard and receding hairline.

Briana stood frozen for a minute then broke the silence by uttering, "Oh, my God!" under her breath. Then she started to giggle and backed away, as though she didn't know how to react. She left me in the bathroom, still holding my old photo. Briana wasn't the only one who was freaked out by me. On the first day of school, I had revealed my family secrets in my class journal. As a result, my teacher, Ms. Neal, didn't know what to make of me either. She obviously felt that my family situation was less than ideal. In fifth grade, when other kids called me a "fat nerd" and I ran sobbing to Ms. Neal, she informed my parents that I had "social problems" that probably related to my "unusual home life," and suggested that I see a counselor. Even at age ten, I was aware of the injustice of her response:

My parents had always taught me to be myself, and I thought other adults would defend me from harassment, not act like it was my fault.

In the long run, Briana eventually came around, after the initial shock wore off. I stayed friends with Lauren and Briana until we graduated on to middle school and made new friends. But from then on I didn't tell any of my friends about my family. I felt like I had enough problems without that additional pressure.

SOME OF MY EARLIEST memories are of my parents fighting. I can remember rocking back and forth in my miniature red rocking chair at the age of three as I watched Jamie and my mom arguing. At one point, I stood up and screamed at them, "Shut up, you big babies!" and ran out of the room. I can't remember what they were fighting about—the sex change, money, work; it seemed like they irritated each other constantly. When I got angry at them for fighting, they would stop for a while, but the peace was uneasy and never lasted for long.

After my parents finally broke up in 1989, my dad had a hard time adjusting. For a while, he would only consume only Cheerios, beer, and coffee-flavored yogurt. On the days I spent with him, he fed me Kid Cuisine–brand TV dinners. Still, we had good moments: Dad started playing the drums, and we spent a lot of time together listening to Elton John and singing at the top of our lungs. Even now, when we listen to the album *Goodbye Yellow Brick Road*, Dad starts smiling and tapping his fingers against the steering wheel.

By the time of the breakup, my Dad's transition from female to male was almost complete, although he continued to make some alterations to his appearance. In 1992, after hiking the John Muir trail for a month, my dad came home with a short, brownish-red beard. At first, I didn't like the beard at all since it made my dad look wildly different, but now I'm used to it.

My father is now a very well-known activist for transsexual rights, and he is often invited to speak at conferences and meetings around the country. I usually refuse to go to these events because, in all honesty, I'm really pretty bored with transsexual things. In addition, I often feel uncomfortable when my dad gets publicity because I don't feel like he is treated with enough respect from the media. A few years ago, for example, there was a large article about him published in a major newspaper that featured a huge picture of him, bare-chested, with a smirk on his face. I thought it made him look like an idiot. The writers of the article wanted to use my real name and current pictures of me (they even offered me money), but I refused, and I'm glad I did. Dad seems to be proud of the articles written about him, or any transsexual for that matter, but I think most of them are sensationalistic, using his life for shock value. At times, I really can't understand why my dad is so obsessed with his own transsexuality.

My dad's life has certainly been radically changed by becoming a transsexual activist, but what matters more to me is that he is still my parent, the person who took care of me as a baby. Once my parents separated we couldn't do the "did today" game at bedtime anymore, but when I have visitation with Dad on Wednesday afternoons, we go out for smoothies at Jamba Juice and talk about all the things that happened that week. Before I was conceived, my maternal grandmother said that she thought only man-woman couples should have children. She loved my parents dearly, but was afraid I'd have an unhappy life because they were in a lesbian relationship. In reality, of course, the only painful times have been caused by other people's prejudices: the times I've worried about telling friends the truth, or the strange, just-what-are-you? looks people gave my dad when he was still making the change.

Grandma (as she now freely admits) was wrong. I love my parents, even if they are freaks. I'm a freak too, and proud.

TRANSLATIONS

Jeffrey Wright, with Christopher Healy

The pages of the black-and-white composition notebook, with loose threads hanging from the binding and a gummy spot on the cover where the price tag used to be, are covered with symbols that look like gibberish. At least that's what most people would think. And that's the idea. Of course, I can read what is written on those lined pages. Those symbols are all part of my alphabet, the one I created years ago to keep my mother from reading things like "When I have more money, I'll go somewhere far away" or "Someday she's going to kill me" or "I am a fag."

PAGE NINETEEN. I'M FOURTEEN years old, with blood trickling down my face in the hallway of our tiny Long Island apartment. I'm listening to my mother tell the cops—whom I had called for help—about how I was being recruited into homosexuality over the World Wide Web. While my mother, with her usual maniacal fervor, presents the computer manuals she calls evidence to the police, I slip into my room to find a new hiding place for my journal. I had managed to stop her before she'd read too far.

The fighting had gotten bad, worse than usual, which is why I'd called 911. I know the police won't do anything about my mom; they never do. But while she's busy explaining how it was all my fault, I need to get my notebook hidden away. I glance quickly around the room, considering a spot underneath the mattress or in the back of the sock drawer before finally stashing it in the sleeve of an old coat hanging in the closet. That will be good enough for now, but I know she'll find it sooner or later during one of her regular room searches. I can't give up writing in the journal, though; it's the only place I feel free to express myself. I just need to come up with a way to keep her from reading the book, even if she finds it—like a secret code of some kind. I decide to start working on it as soon as things calm down here. I step back out into the hallway to see my brother Mike, who has just arrived, telling the police, "Don't listen to Jeff, man. He's a little liar."

The next day, I start writing with an alphabet of my own creation: backward letters, geometric shapes, picture-style hieroglyphs. They each stand for a separate sound, and strung together they form words. My thoughts and feelings are safe now, disguised from my mother and my brother and anyone else who might use them against me.

By page twenty-three I'm lying in a hospital bed, watching the shapes around me come in and out of focus. I'm not sure if the fogginess I'm feeling is the result of the drugs they're pumping into me or the blows to the head I've received. I can make out my mother just beyond the IV machine and Mike by the doorway. Mike's head hangs down, and I can't tell for sure, but he looks sad. The look on his face now is miles away from the way he looked a few hours earlier, as he straddled me on the floor and brought down his fists over and over.

Page thirty-one. I walk into the apartment, coming home from my job at the restaurant, and I hear Mike screaming from the other room. Mom is yelling, too; their mingled voices are unintelligible. I hear the loud smack of flesh on flesh. There's nothing I can do. I go into my room and close the door.

Page thirty-three. I'm in a noisy crowded corridor in my high school, pretending to be looking for something in my locker when in actuality I'm watching a group of seniors out of the corner of my eye: four guys in tight T-shirts and baggy jeans They laugh and slap each other on the back. I wish I was part of their group. And more, I want to feel their touch.

I shuffle through the papers in my backpack, stalling until I have to get to my next class. The bell rings and, as the hallway clears, three of the guys take off, but the fourth stays. His hair is black and very short. He has a strong jawline. He looks at his watch and sits down cross-legged on the floor. He's beautiful. I want to watch him for hours. He leans his head back against the wall and closes his eyes, and I wonder what he's waiting for. I consider asking him, but I know I can't just walk up and start talking to a guy I don't know. I don't want him to think I'm gay. And I'm late for class, anyway. I close my locker and dash off to math.

Not long after—maybe a few days and four or five journal pages—my mother comes after me again. I see the gleam of the knife in my mother's hand as it arcs toward me. I feel the pain in my side as I slide across the kitchen floor and reach into the silverware drawer for a knife of my own. I am scared. But beyond that, I am angry. We square off, eye to eye, each with a weapon in hand.

Page fifty-two. Months pass. I am fifteen, padding quietly down the aisle of a gay bookstore. I'm following the tall green-eyed guy with muscular shoulders into the back room. He flashes me a smile and shuts the door behind me. Soon I feel his strong hands on my sides and his thighs press against mine. I slide my hand up his back, under his shirt, trembling at the feel of his skin. We don't say anything. My head rests briefly on his chest before I look back into his beautiful eyes. At last, I know who I am.

I flip through the next dozen or so pages, past the numerous hour-long train trips to New York, past harsh words and swollen bruises, past the French boy and the German boy, and I stop at page seventy-one, the night I make the phone call to my friend Carla. I tell her about this guy Jay I'd met. I giggle, confiding to her how the romantic evening Jay and I had planned turned into a fire drill after the candles we'd lit set off the smoke alarms in his apartment. We're laughing about it until I hear a click on the line and realize my mother has picked up the other phone. In the time it takes me to fully comprehend what she's just heard, she bursts into my room, arms flailing. She screams about how sick I am and rips the phone from my hand. I see the fury in her bulging eyes and quivering lip and I tense myself for the blows I know are about to come. But she doesn't hit me this time. She stares at me with disgust and walks out.

That same night, at just about 3:00 A.M., I pull the zipper shut on the last of the four bags into which I've packed everything that's mine. I secure all the bags over my shoulders and give one more test tug to the rope I've got tied around the foot of my bed and hanging out the window. It seems tight. Trying hard to move silently, I climb out the window and start my descent down the rope. Halfway down, there's a sharp jerk as the bed moves an inch. I shimmy the rest of the way to the ground in sheer panic, far less afraid of falling than I am of my mother hearing me leave. I hit the pavement on my feet, and run straight to the train station. It is my sixteenth birthday.

Page eighty-nine. It's weeks later and I'm in Connecticut, shocked out of sleep by a ringing phone. Jon rolls over and picks up the receiver. It's Jon's bed. Jon's apartment. I am so thankful for Jon.

After running away, I'd spent a night in a crowded Covenant House shelter in Manhattan. The next day, I wandered into a random restaurant and discovered Jon, a college student, who was alone, aimlessly fiddling with the Sweet 'N Low packages on his table as though he was waiting for someone to talk to. I shared my story, and, grasping both my hands across the table, he told me that I could come stay with him. And so now here I am, in the middle of the night, watching Jon sit up sharply in the bed as he listens to the person on the other end of the line. I know it's my mother; I never should have told her where I was in the first place. I just wanted her to forward my mail.

Her voice is so brash and loud I can hear it from where I am. I push the covers back and slide sheepishly from the bed, feigning a need to go to the bathroom. I don't want to hear Jon defend me again. I feel so bad for dragging him into this, putting him directly in my mother's line of fire. I had assumed that once I was gone, she'd be happy to be rid of me. Countless visits from the police, calls from the FBI, and even letters from the governor's office, have proven otherwise. She's not going to stop. I run the water in the bathroom sink, because I feel like I'm going to start crying and I don't want Jon to hear it, but suddenly he's standing in the doorway. "She's got someone there who says he's going to come after me," Jon says. "We've got to do something."

And so, we decide to do the only thing that makes any sense. We go to court. On page 112, I'm in the courtroom tugging nervously at my borrowed tie, waiting for the judge to come back with his verdict. Sara, the lawyer that Jon found for me, puts her hand on my shoulder and gives me a reassuring smile. She's much more confident than I am that things will turn out all right. I have such a hard time truly believing that my mother's influence over me could actually come to an end. Throughout the entire trial, I've struggled not to look at my mother. I didn't want to see her face while Sara described all the physical abuse and mental torture I'd been put through and argued to the judge that the only reason my mother wanted me back was to insure her continued child support payments from the state. I hold my breath as the judge reenters, approaches the bench, and asks my mother and me and our respective lawyers to stand. After all this, if I have to go back, I might as well kill myself; I'll be dead in a matter of days anyway. The judge clears his throat and reads his decision, declaring my legal emancipation from my mother. The air bursts violently from my lungs and I grip the edge of the table in front of me to keep from falling over. I never have to see my mother again.

By page 117, the joy of my freedom has diminished. I sit by the window in Jon's apartment, staring out at a gray sky. Jon is in the bedroom with the door shut. I'd left him in there, walking out halfway through the argument and shutting the door behind me, because I didn't want to let it escalate. Jon and I both care about each other, but I don't think either of us is ready to be living with a partner full time. Our tolerance for one another seems to be growing thin. We need time apart. I decide to take my new friend Alexander up on his offer and fly down to Atlanta for a few days.

I met Alexander about fifty pages earlier in my journal, months

before the trial. He called me up at Jon's apartment out of no-
where. He said his name was Alexander and explained how he
got my number. A few days earlier, I'd been strolling among
the purple perms and linebacker-size evening dresses of Wigs-
tock, the gay Mardi Gras, and I passed my name and number
off to a really cute guy, who apparently gave it to this guy,
Alexander. He's an older man, old enough to be my dad, and
I have no idea why he wants to talk to me. It doesn't take me
long, though, to realize he's not trying to hit on me; he just
wants to talk. He's had some really bad stuff happen to him
and he tells me about it all very bluntly: his parents had just
died, and he'd lost a lot of good friends to AIDS, including a
guy he'd been in a long relationship with, whom he'd believed
to be his one true love. Alexander's openness makes me trust
him almost immediately and I tell him my story—all of it.

Scanning through the pages from this point, I come across
dozens of entries recounting phone conversations with Alexander. In all of them I come home sore and tense from working
three jobs or from hearing my mother testify about me in a
courtroom all day, and I get on the phone with Alexander and
he eases me through it all. He makes me aware of my own
strength, and it gives me hope until the next day. With every
phone call we grow closer, until one day, at our first face-to-
face meeting, he extends an open invitation for me to go down
to his home in Atlanta for a visit.

PAGE 122. WE JUST had dinner together, Alexander and I. We
ate, we talked, we laughed. No harsh words were exchanged.
Nobody made me feel uncomfortable or unwanted. Halfway
through the meal, I looked down at my hand to see the inden-
tations in my palm from gripping my fork so tightly. I'd been
ready for a fight, but none came.

Page 123. I'm sitting up in bed in the room Alexander set
up for me, writing in my journal for the night. Suddenly, I hear
someone at the door. I jump back with a start, shoving the
notebook under the covers. It's Alexander at the door. "Good
night," he says.

Page 125. I feel safe and loved, to the extent I know what that means.

Page 126. I'm standing by the car with my bags as Alexander says good-bye to his friend Craig before driving me back to the airport. Alexander gives Craig a hug and steps back to open the car door for me. As I throw my bags in the backseat, I hear Alexander's friend say, "You guys are so great together. I don't know why Jeff doesn't stay and be your son."

Page 130. I'm back in Atlanta, two weeks into what we determined to be a "trial adoption." I wasn't sure who was more frightened by the prospect, me or Alexander, but we both decided we owed it to ourselves to at least give it a try. I am not looking for a new family. I was so happy to be rid of the first one. But something about Alexander seems right. We sit on his sofa watching *Auntie Mame*, the five o'clock movie. Alexander compares me to the little boy in the movie and himself to Auntie Mame, and I can't help but smile.

Page 134. We're riding the tram at Six Flags. Alexander, wearing a big floppy Dr. Seuss hat, jumps from his seat and begins to dance a goofy little jig. He motions to me, and I hop up from my seat to join him, the bells on my jester's cap jingling. The two of us high-step it down the aisle to the delight and bewilderment of onlooking passengers. Out of breath, we stop in a grand pose and take our bows. There is only a smattering of applause from the other passengers, but that doesn't matter. Alexander envelops me in a hug, and the two of us sit back down to enjoy the rest of the ride. I feel like slowly and belatedly, I'm getting a real childhood. It seems too good to last.

Pages later, just as I feared, this good thing, too, is starting to fall apart. Alexander stands across the room, staring at me silently. The crystal paperweight I just threw across the room lies chipped on the floor by the bookshelf. With my eyes watering up, I run past Alexander to my room. I can't remember what started the argument, what set me off. This is not what I want to happen. I sit on the edge of my bed and wait for my heart to stop racing. When I can focus again, I go back into the other room. Alexander is waiting for me. He gives me the chance to speak first. "I'm sorry," I say. "I just need time."

Page 139: the Fourth of July. With the sounds of fireworks booming in the sky as our backdrop, Alexander and I prepare to cast a "magic spell." Alexander's friend Craig has just left us after moping around all night, talking about how unlucky he is in love. Now Alexander and I thought we'd try to help him out and have a little fun in the process. Alexander runs his finger down a page in a book entitled *Love Hexes*, checking off a list of ingredients. As Alexander reads off the ingredients, I place them all into a little jewelry box, one by one: a hair from Craig's head (conveniently found on the sofa where he'd been sitting), Craig's name written in red on a piece of blue paper, some wax from a red candle, a single rose petal. The two of us read aloud an odd little chant from the book and place the box under my bed. I smile and think how nice it would be if that weird love hex actually helped Craig find happiness. And then I wonder if anybody has cast a spell for me.

Page 141. I've never been to Savannah and I've decided I want to go. I look at the clock. It's six, I can still catch a late bus. I pack a small bag and tell Alexander I'm leaving. I'm completely taken aback by his response. He doesn't want me to go. It's too late; it's not safe; he goes on and on. I bark back at him. I can't have someone controlling my life. If he wants to take me on, I'm ready. But as I yell, I look deep into Alexander's eyes and I realize that it's not anger fueling his words, but concern. He's not my mother. I catch my breath and lower my voice. "I'm sorry," I say. "I just need time alone. I need to be able to get away sometimes. Like when I used to go to New York to be alone. Don't worry, I'm coming back." Alexander drives me to the bus terminal.

Page 146. A shock runs through my entire body as I overhear the two men at the bar hypothesizing about Alexander and me being lovers. We're at a gay club. These guys are queers, too, why wouldn't they trust us? One of them calls Alexander a pedophile. The other chuckles, takes a sip of his margarita, and agrees, saying there's something just a little too kinky about our living arrangement. I run to find Alexander to tell him what I've overheard. I'm disgusted, not only by the lack of faith these guys obviously have in us, but also at the idea of having sex with my father. I stop in my tracks, amid a crowd of dancers, and take in the sudden realization that I think of Alexander as my *father*. My first father, ever.

Page 150. I'm back in Connecticut and on the phone with Alexander in Georgia. "I'm scared," I say to him. "I'm scared, too," he replies. But I can't deny the longing to be back with him that I've felt ever since I left Atlanta. I'm still not sure I want to be part of a family, but he is the only person who's ever really felt like family to me. I tell Alexander all of this. He's smiling on the other end; I can hear the smile in his voice. He tells me to come back, that he would like to adopt me. I hang up the phone and quickly pack my bags so I can go back to live with my father.

Page 162. I sit next to Alexander at the huge round table in the Mexican restaurant. All of our friends surround us, joking and laughing. They all came when I called. Alexander adjusts the striped pointy hat on his head as I lead the group in a chorus of "Happy Birthday." As the song comes to a ridiculously off-key finale, Alexander flashes me a big, goofy smile, puts his hand on my shoulder, and turns to blow out the candles. I made the right choice.

Before I shut the book for the night, I turn back to page ninety-nine. I'm in a small Italian restaurant in Greenwich Village. After weeks of getting to know each other over the phone, this is the first time Alexander and I meet in person. We sit across from each other. Alexander has my journal open in front of him. I reach past the water glasses and little pats of butter to point to the various symbols of my alphabet, explaining how each is pronounced. "Thank you," Alexander says. I watch him sound out the words on the page and realize that, strangely enough, I am not at all afraid that there is now someone else who has full access to my secret thoughts and dreams. I want it to be this way. I want Alexander to be the one other person on this earth who can read my life.

I close the book.

SMILE AND SAY NOTHING

Ian Wheeler-Nicholson

O n a September morning about twenty years ago, I stood rocking back and forth impatiently, nervously, on the front lawn
of our house while my mother buttoned up my jacket for the
first day at my new school. I was used to the routine. Every
summer we would move to a new town and I would enroll in
a new elementary school, having to memorize whole classrooms
full of children who had shot spitballs at each other since pre-
school. I was well acquainted with the hostility of children to
newcomers, and so, once again, I had the jitters.

"Now, listen," my mother said, taking me a little roughly
by the shoulders, so that I'd pay attention. "If anybody asks
you where your father is or who you live with, don't tell them
anything." And with these quick and cryptic words, she pushed
me, confused now as well as nervous, down the path to the
school bus.

My mother had never been good at communication. She was
a reserved woman who kept her secrets to herself. On this occasion, however, I sensed that she was trying to tell me something important. I had no idea what it could be.

I stood awkwardly at the bus stop with a group of six or
seven other children, some in fourth grade like me, others as
old as sixth graders. They talked furiously among themselves
about summer camp and Boy Scouts and cast suspicious
glances at me. A couple of the boys started an energetic game
of catch with a worn-out softball but did not invite me to
participate. With my mother's strange warning still ringing in

my ears, I was nervous that somebody would approach me suddenly and ask me, "Where's your father? Who lives at your house?" although I didn't know why these questions should be feared.

Finally, a long yellow school bus arrived, driven by an old, pockmarked man who looked like Popeye. The seats were upholstered in green vinyl, marked with graffiti like *DISCO SUCKS* and *LED ZEP 4-EVER!* and packed with screaming, giggling children. Frenzied at the start of a new school year, most of them were busy throwing papers and pencils back and forth. I didn't know anyone, of course, and so I chose a seat in front, near the bus driver, thereby officially establishing myself as an outsider. It is an unspoken rule of school buses that the more popular you are, the farther toward the back you sit.

On the way to school, sitting self-conscious and alone in the front of the bus while chaos ruled the seats behind me, I thought about what my mother had said. But why would anyone care where my father was? He was in New York City, where he had lived since my parents divorced when I was an infant. I had no memory of their ever having been married, in fact, and privately doubted that such an absurd thing could be true. And whom did I live with? My mother, of course, and Veronica, a woman around my mother's age with whom she shared a bedroom. Veronica wasn't my family, but she had always been there, at least as long as I could remember.

We had moved to our new town just a few weeks earlier, in the waning weeks of August. It was a small, working-class New Jersey suburb near the shore, overshadowed by a more affluent community to the north. We knew nobody in town except the Realtor. Our street was a bland, modern development of ranchstyle houses with identical green lawns. From the large picture window, I had watched groups of children passing by on bicycles or playing together in neighbors' yards, but being shy, I had not gone up to them. My constant moves from town to town had left me without close friends but at least had given me the ability to amuse myself without playmates.

My first glimpse of my new school was not promising. My

mother had been struggling financially since the divorce, and this was a poor town with a school to match. Our school, constructed in the late fifties, was a big institutional rectangle planted on a patch of grass between a highway to the east and an electric utility company to the west. It was painted a dingy beige color, and the facade was chipped and cracking. The barely tended grass on the front lawn was brown after the hot summer.

My bus pulled up into a line of others in the long driveway in front of the school's imposing front doors. Hundreds of kids were milling around the steps. Filing from the bus with the others, I caught glimpses of boys in the fifth and sixth grades, and they seemed enormous and definitely threatening. It was the late seventies, so many of the older boys had long hair and wore patch logos of classic rock bands on their denim jackets. By contrast, I felt small and weak in my creased plaid shirt and tan corduroys.

That first day passed almost without incident, until the end of the day, when I learned a new word that would eventually explain many of the questions I had, not only about my mother's command that morning, but also about our constant moves from town to town.

I was walking down one of the long, unfamiliar halls of the school at 3:00 P.M., alone, with some new textbooks under my arm, thinking about going home, where I could be alone and at peace with my toys and TV set, the consolations of being an only child. As I came to the big doors that led outside, I passed a group of three older boys leaning against the wall. They saw me coming and, pegging me as a new kid, stepped into my path.

"Hey, check out this dweeb," said one, a tall boy with long blond hair and a scruffy flannel shirt over jeans with holes in the knees.

"Yeah, what a dork," said another with cigarette breath and a face full of zits. I looked at them nervously, and waited.

"So, you little geek," said the blond one, leaning down into my face, "which do you like, rock or disco?"

"What?" My face, against all the effort I could muster, was heating up and must have been a brilliant fuchsia.

"Come on, man," he taunted. "It's a simple question. Rock or disco?"

I didn't know what to say. I knew rock and disco were different kinds of music, but I didn't know much more about them. My idea of music at that time was the Broadway soundtrack to *Annie*, which I had on a double LP and knew by heart, though I wouldn't have admitted this. A song called "Le Freak" had come out that year, which I had heard on the radio and thought was pretty cool, and which I believed was disco. Yet somehow I had a sense this would be the wrong answer. I thought back to my morning on the bus, and the words scrawled on a nearby seat: *DISCO SUCKS.*

"Rock," I said. "Disco sucks!"

The boys seemed pleased with this response.

"That's right, dude," the blond boy said. "Make sure you listen to rock. Only faggots like disco!"

They stepped aside, and I hurried on my way, but as I got back on the bus, I was already wondering: *What were faggots?*

It didn't take me long to find out. In this new, rougher school, I began hearing playground slang previously unknown to me. Among the tough Irish and Italian boys of this working-class town, "homo" and "faggot" were the worst sort of insults one boy could throw at another. It was understood that calling a boy a faggot was serious, the kind of remark that makes other kids shut up and wait to see what happens.

What the word actually meant was not clear to me at first, but I soon came to understand that it referred to a peculiar species of man that had sex with other men. The whole concept of sex itself was just breaking over my consciousness at this period, and it seemed absurd and grotesque enough without this added information. As easily disgusted and titillated as boys my age were by anything grossly sexual, we were reduced to hysterics at the idea of faggots.

There was more. These words, *faggot* and *homo*, were only supposed to be used in reference to men. There were special words for women: *dyke* and *lesbo*. This latter one was apparently short for some longer term, vaguely scientific, but I didn't learn that word, with its strangely classical connotations, until later. The idea was clear, however. Dykes were freaks, women who did it with women.

Accusations would fly at any female who wasn't girlie enough. Whenever a girl showed any guy tendencies—a good throwing arm or perspiration—she could be branded a dyke. Ironically, every now and then, a girl who was ultrafeminine might be considered dykey, too. For example, I remember a group of boys taunting a girl as a "lesbo" during gym class one day because she was not only exceptionally good at softball but also had begun to grow breasts.

This business about dykes cut a little close. After working out just what a dyke was, I remember feeling an uncomfortable coldness in my chest. Along with my rudimentary understanding of the mechanics of sex, I had stumbled upon an uncomfortable truth: my mother, apparently, was a dyke. Suddenly, when she came home from work, I looked at her with a mixture of fear and embarrassment. I knew something about her that nobody else knew, something that was wrong, at least according to the conventional wisdom.

Maybe it was an indication of the distance between me and my mother in those days that I didn't ask her about any of this. Looking back, I can see that my mother was going through a hard time herself, trying to find a new identity after years of an unsatisfying "straight" marriage. Her ability to provide emotional reassurance to me was limited, and her attention to the details of parenting was sometimes perfunctory. Only later, when she had achieved a greater degree of self-acceptance, could she look at me and see how I was doing. But when I was ten years old, I had no one to turn to for advice on dealing with gay people or those who hated them.

What was obvious to me—as it had been to my mother—was that I had to keep the fact of her lesbianism a complete secret. As a new kid, neither rich nor athletic, I was already at a disadvantage in this town; if people learned that my mother lived and slept with another woman, my fragile reputation would be finished, and I would likely be in for a serious whupping.

One particular incident taught me the importance of keeping silent about what went on in my house. The only boy in class who was smaller and more outwardly effeminate than me was Frederick, an almost pretty boy with blue eyes and very blond hair. He had an exuberant personality, was full of energy, and was a favorite of the teachers. He was sweet, friendly, and cheerful and even went out of his way to ask my name and say hi to me when we ran into one another in the hall, for which I was grateful.

Naturally, the other boys didn't like him. For one thing, he had too many friends who were girls. Frederick seemed more content chatting with girls in home ec class than any boy had a right to be. He was also popular in arts-and-crafts class, exhibiting skill in painting and drawing and building that odd child-brand of folk art from household items—collages made of pine cones and geodesic domes made of Popsicle sticks.

It was one of those classes, in fact, that proved to be Frederick's undoing. One afternoon, after arts and crafts, we were all filing out through the open-air courtyard in the center of the school, holding our crafts projects, and Frederick was talking animatedly with a group of his girlfriends about his painting project, which had won praise from our teacher. He had painted a landscape scene with people in it, and he had correctly used perspective, so that the people in the distance were smaller than the people in the foreground. I personally thought it was brilliant and far outshone my own feeble effort. At any rate, a group of four or five boys gathered nearby noticed Frederick, shining with pride in the middle of a group of girls, and must have been deeply offended.

"Hey, check out the fag," one of them said.

Frederick looked up, instantly on guard. He was wearing bright blue pants and a red striped T-shirt, bursting with color compared to the mean-faced surly boys in their identical ripped T-shirts and blue jeans and long hair.

"Yeah," said another, trying to grab Frederick's painting. "Little homo's good at art, huh? What you got there, fag?"

They gathered around him, trying to snatch his painting away, but he was a nimble kid and managed to keep it out of their hands. His pack of girlfriends slunk away, frightened. I lurked nearby, behind a trash can, watching, as did some others. We could see what was about to happen: Frederick had been targeted, there were no grown-ups around, and it wasn't going to be pretty.

Frederick shouted indignantly that they leave him alone, but the boys were having fun. He held his own against them for a while, but his face was red and he looked scared. It was a hot, sunny fall day, and a sense of restlessness ran through the students, who were still thinking about the summer vacation just past. One of the big boys finally grabbed Frederick's painting.

"Aw, lookit what a pretty picture!"

"Gimme that back," shouted Frederick.

The boy looked at him with dead eyes, challenging: "Make me, you little faggot."

Frederick leaped at his attacker and kicked him in the shin, hard. That was it. In an instant, all the boys were on Frederick at once. It was fast and brutal. I was shocked. I had seen fights before, but they had always been between two boys, usually two of the bigger boys, butting heads like a pair of rams. This was different; it was calculated and violent. I couldn't see what was happening—there were too many bodies in the way and children gathered around, yelling, "Fight! Fight!"

In seconds, adults appeared to drag the boys apart, still waving their fists and shouting, "Get him! Get the little homo!" Frederick was bloody and pale. The boys had punched him and kicked him from all sides at once. His pretty face was covered in the clay dust of the courtyard, and a stream of blood was gushing from his nostrils and the corner of his mouth. He was carried off by a female teacher to the nurse's office, leaving a trail of bright red drops in the dust, while the big boys were marched away to detention by a small army of assistant principals. I slipped away, unnoticed.

After this beating, Frederick became withdrawn and shy, sitting by himself at lunch and sneaking off after school. And then, after two weeks or so, he simply disappeared. He was

soon forgotten by just about everyone. But not by me. I understood that the incident I had witnessed could easily have involved me. Frederick and I, in the eyes of the other children,
were guilty of the same crime: not being boy enough. We were
both bad at sports and good at art. I was, like Frederick, a little
small for my age. This had been enough for Frederick to be
branded "faggot," and his mother wasn't even a dyke.

NOW I KNEW WHAT my mother had been afraid of: that, in my
innocence, I would give away information that might get me
into trouble. "Oh, my dad's gone, and I live with two women."
She had been right to warn me. In those days, in that town,
homosexuals had one choice: keep silent and hope nobody finds
out. My mother never wanted to make me complicit in her own
personal deception, but she simply had no choice.

And so a cloud of invisibility settled over our little ranch
house on our little street of identical lawns. We were the neighbors nobody ever saw. My mother and Veronica commuted to
work in other towns and made no connections among our
neighbors. I had no friends. I had never been popular anyway,
always being a newcomer, not to mention introverted and a
little weird, so it was not too difficult to avoid other kids and
their uncomfortable questions.

There were inconveniences, of course, to this secretive life.
Halloween, for example—the one day on which neighbors who
otherwise never speak to one another persist in dragging their
costumed children up and down the street, ringing doorbells for
miniature Mr. Goodbars and Skittles—was awkward. It would
not do for a group of children and mothers dressed as witches
and vampires to come to our door and see our little domestic
scene: Two Women and a Baby. It became our family tradition
to go out to dinner and then to a movie on Halloween, not
returning to our home until the neighborhood ghouls had been
safely tucked in.

Still, generally, my routine was simple: I would go to school,
say as little as possible, and go home, where I would play by

myself, imagination overcompensating for the absence of playmates. I learned to become invisible, unremarkable. I drew attention to myself neither by my dress nor by my behavior nor
by my academic performance. Attention invited questions.

My tactic worked. Though I was thought a little strange,
nobody bothered with me beyond an occasional mocking. I
stayed quiet and so managed to avoid provoking the kind of
attention that Frederick had brought on himself. When people
did speak to me, teachers or students, I would simply smile and
say nothing.

Without knowing it, I had stumbled on my mother's very
own solution to the problem of leading a covert homosexual
life. In later years, she would tell me that the main reason for
our constant moves was that, in each place, eventually a nosy
neighbor or a coworker would begin to suspect the truth about
my mother or her partner. My mother was always afraid of
losing her job, and there was the looming threat of violence.
And so we became an itinerant family.

The irony of all this for me, of course, was that I was not
gay myself. In fact, I was, as far as I could tell, pretty much like
other boys, sexually speaking. Certainly, as the next few years
passed and I approached adolescence, I began to notice details
about girls in a way I never had before—their nascent breasts,
their long hair and clear skin. But this didn't matter. My mother
made me different.

What was always strange to me was that, as far as I could
tell, my life was so unobjectionable—even boring. I spent my
evenings watching TV, reading comic books, or playing with
toys while mom and Veronica cooked or watched the news.
Sometimes on a Saturday we'd go to the mall or the movies
together. On summer evenings, Veronica liked to barbecue in
the backyard, which was screened by trees from the prying eyes
of neighbors. If it was too hot, we'd drive to the Baskin-Robbins
in the next town for ice cream. In the absence of a father, it
was Veronica who taught me how to throw a football (which
I never did very well) and how to ride a two-wheeled bike
(which I did somewhat better).

As far as their sex went, it happened behind closed doors, as I suppose it does in most straight households, and was of no interest to me whatsoever. It was years before I was even conclusively sure that they had sex. Later, when I became a teenager and started dating girls, my mother greeted my burgeoning heterosexuality not with hostility but with the mix of apprehension and pride common, most likely, to all mothers.

But the constant awareness that the world outside was our enemy took its toll. My mother clearly suffered stress from keeping her identity secret. She could sometimes be harsh, cold, and impatient, as could Veronica, engaged in similar struggles. There's no way to prevent the anxiety of deception from seeping into a family's daily life.

As for me, I suffered knowing that I was considered somehow different and wrong, though I had done nothing to merit this. I became depressed, angry, and frustrated. I saw how other children seemed to live by the exclamation point—"Give me!" "I want!"—while I was ruled by the question mark—"Why don't people like me?" "What have I done?"

Eventually, the situation got better. When I was fifteen, my mother's new job allowed us to abandon the restrictive culture of our small town life for the wider freedom and tolerance of the city. In the urbane environment of my city school, I could be more open about my family, and, for the first time, make friends.

As for my mother, though we long ago escaped the frightening confines of the parochial suburbs, she has spent the two decades since then in corporate America, another kind of masquerade, in which homosexuality, while perhaps no longer legally a firing offense, is nevertheless not good for one's career. Her cloak of invisibility has never quite been shed.

Some time ago, I was visiting my mother for lunch at her office, when one of her female coworkers came in with a gossipy story about another woman's husband and his misbehavior. "Oh, but you know how men are," the woman concluded, and looked to my mother for reassurance. My mother simply smiled and said nothing, just as I had seen her do a thousand times before.

FATHER'S DAY

Maria De La O

I t was 10:00 A.M. on June seventh when the phone rang. I
didn't bother to screen the call. I knew exactly who it was.

"Have you thought about what you're giving for Father's
Day yet?" Robert, my father's live-in spouse—or between the
two of us, Robertoria, Ms. Roberta, Miss Thang, the Wicked
Stepmother—always liked a good conspiracy to surprise my
father.

Of course, I didn't have any gifts planned yet. Besides being
notoriously disorganized, I was a busy woman. I hadn't even
been living in Manhattan a year yet, and already my ten-to-ten
job as a web site producer had made the daily details of living
virtually impossible to keep up with.

"Do you have any ideas?" I queried on cue. Robert liked to
be a fussbudget mama bear, fretting about my father's creeping
waistline and the starch in his shirt collars. He played the part
with a healthy dose of ironic camp, but he also truly reveled in
the role. And with my father for a mate, he had the perfect foil:
a manly-man who owned an electrical contracting company,
drank Bud Light instead of Northern California microbrew, and
counted never turning on the heat in the winter (preferring to
build fires) as a point of pride.

"Done," Robert said, and excitedly told me about his find:
a T-shirt with the slogan "San Francisco Fire Department"
which my dad had been eyeing for over a month in the window
of Husbands, a Castro neighborhood boutique. I was relieved
that I didn't have to worry about a gift, and besides, I was
always excited to talk to Robertoria. We spent the rest of our

conversation catching up on the usual: me complaining about my boss, Cruella; him advising me to tell Ms. De Vil to take a flying leap. (Robert knew the subject of my boss well; he'd had the misfortune of answering the phone the previous Christmas Day to Cruella's very-merry inquiries about my latest column for the web site.)

Robert also asked about my girlfriend, Ms. Alice, and whether she had gotten tired of New York University so we could move back to the Left Coast. He informed me that my dad was working way too hard—as usual.

Robertoria didn't mention that he himself had finally stopped going to work altogether or that he spent most of his hours racked by migraines. And, cheerful as ever, he certainly didn't mention that this phone call might be the most strenuous task he would accomplish that day. We ended the conversation the way we always did, with smooch noises and an affectionate "Ciao-ciao," Italian-style.

I had no idea that this would be one of the last times Robert would play Wicked Stepmother to my Harried Working Girl. I didn't know this would be one of the last times I would speak to him. I didn't realize, as I hung up the phone and contemplated how much work I would have to slog through over the next week, that a few months later, Robert would die from AIDS-related complications, just before protease inhibitors appeared on the scene.

WHEN I MET ROBERT, my relationship with my dad was neither particularly close nor distant; it was uninteresting, neutral, and somehow typical. My mother and father had gotten divorced when I was four, after my mother's shocked discovery that my father was not having sex with just her, but with one of his male friends as well. My father abruptly moved away from San Diego, and I didn't see him again until he came back when I was eight. Soon, we eased into the every-other-weekend-with-dad routine so popular with family court judges.

I think my dad wanted us to be closer. He took me camping

and fishing, until I unequivocally declared that I hated wilderness sports and, as though to prove my point, accidentally dropped my fishing pole in the middle of the lake. Every now and then, he would tote me along to his deadly dull job sites, and I would keep myself occupied by reading *Mad* magazine or sorting tools. During the holiday season, he and I planned a craft project—stained glass one year, silk-screening another—to give to friends and relatives. We spent our weekends together laboring on those gifts from mid-October until Christmas morning. Despite the stress that sometimes ensued after dipping thirty-seven candles, I liked the idea of making my own Christmas presents—and working alongside my dad.

Once in a while he would tell me lesson-stories: how the kids at school made fun of him because he had hair on his chest before the rest of the boys did (translation: I understand your concern about breast development, dear). But he never said anything about who he dated or why he and mom got divorced. In fact, there was only one time that he brought up anything gay at all.

I was nearly ten, and we were putt-putting along in my dad's VW van when he spontaneously launched into the story of Harvey Milk, the San Francisco city supervisor who had just been killed. He told me how Mr. Milk had been shot and that lots of people were sad and very angry. I knew that he was telling me this because it was somehow important and historical. He told me that Harvey Milk was gay, too. I nodded. I knew what gay meant but wasn't sure why such a thing would make any difference.

Despite our heavy talks and crafts projects, I don't think I ever really forgave my dad for what I considered his abandonment of our little family. During those four years he was away, when curious playmates wanted to know where my dad was, I would say that my parents were divorced. And if they were one of those kids who still didn't know what divorce was, I found it easier to say that I didn't have a father.

My father had hurt my mom with his behavior, too. When she discovered him in bed with his friend, she abruptly whisked me away to her parents' house. We returned only once to gather our things. Later on, after the papers were signed, she began to hurl insults about "that queer," often after a session of pleading with him to send child-support checks or arguing with him over where I would spend Thanksgiving or, at times, for no reason at all.

I don't think my mother was antigay because of any intrinsic belief system. I think she was anti–my father. Still, on many occasions, I overheard my mother saying that gay people were bad enough, and bisexuals were even worse. She couldn't have known that, years later, those words would still ring in my ears.

THIS IS HOW ROBERTORIA and my father got together.

During my first year at the University of California at Berkeley, my father came up from San Diego to drag me to my cousin John's wedding in a nearby suburb. The next day, on his way back to the airport, he ventured across the bridge to San Francisco for a pit-stop drink.

It was a Sunday, and barely noon, so there was hardly anyone in the Pilsner, which was then a semi-seedy joint on the edge of the Castro. My father was ensconced at the bar, and nursing a beer when Robert sauntered in with his morning *Chronicle* and sat down on a neighboring empty stool. My dad, playing the smart-ass—or was he flirting?—stole a glance at him and said, "That seat's taken." As Robert began gathering his newspaper, my dad smiled and told him to go ahead and sit down.

They talked nonstop for the next two hours, right up until my dad had to catch the 3:30 shuttle to SoCal. Soon, he and Robert began calling each other long distance nearly every day, racking up hours and hours of conversation. Perhaps they never would have realized it was true love if Robert hadn't worked for the phone company.

This was something new for my dad. He wasn't the kind of guy to meet someone at a bar and launch into a torrid relationship. As a matter of fact, I had never noticed him having relationships at all, or even dating. My dad had male house-mates, but they had their own rooms, and I never saw anything sexual—not so much as a hug—so I could never tell whether or not anything was *really* going on.

As a result, despite my mother's adamant and vitriolic claims, I never totally believed that my father was gay. He wasn't the way I thought gay people were supposed to be—nelly and limp-wristed and certainly not construction workers! It's not that I thought my mother would lie about such a thing, but being gay seemed like a very serious charge, something you ought to have evidence for. Finally, when I was about thirteen, my dad mentioned that he was, indeed, gay. The comment was made almost in passing, to someone else. It was anticlimactic, but it was the conclusive proof I had been hoping for.

After the information had sunk in, I felt so alone. I felt confused and panicked as questions roiled around inside my head. I already felt that I was very different from everyone else I knew at school. I was already slow in the breast development department. And I was a "gifted" kid—the social kiss of death. Now I had a gay dad, too.

And mixed in with those thoughts was the seed of something else: Dad hadn't seemed gay, but he was. Could I be gay, too?

THROUGH MOST OF HIGH school, I kept the issue firmly tucked away in the back of my mind, until it came bursting out near the end of senior year, when I fell for my best girl friend over too many cups of coffee and angst-ridden discussions.

Still, I never said a word about my infatuation to anyone, except for Jack, a boy I latched onto as soon as I realized I was attracted to girls. One night, after Jack and I had had sex, I somewhat nervously said, "Y'know, I think I'm bisexual."

"Um, I think I am, too," he replied, and proceeded to tell me about his late-night forays into the park, looking for men. Jack's reaction surprised me and calmed my anxiety. Maybe being bisexual was really not such a big deal, after all.

The next summer, just after freshman year of college, I met

Angela, a cook at a vegetarian restaurant who trained me on the grill. We were a little different: I was sporty and collegiate looking in T-shirts and shorts; Angela constantly chewed tooth-picks and boasted a wardrobe of leather and chains. We regularly worked the Sunday breakfast shift together, mock-insulting each other all the while. I started giving her rides home from work, and eventually she suggested going out together some evening.

I was another notch in her spike-encrusted belt; she shook up my otherwise bland summer. And after Angela showed me off at her ex-girlfriend's party, she stopped returning my phone calls *and* coming to work.

Of course, my dad hadn't a clue about my burgeoning sex-uality. We didn't talk about those sorts of things. I mean, he was my *dad*. He reminded me to write thank-you cards. He gave advice on which classes to take at school (which I ignored). Besides, I had only just started having sex with boys in the last year or two. I could be going through an experimental stage! Certainly, I wasn't going to start making any announcements.

But my father was.

When I saw him with Robert for the first time, it changed everything. Robert was attractive, friendly ("I've heard so much about you!" he exclaimed with a wide smile) and *boy*, was he gay. Actually, I had never seen my dad with someone so gay. Adorned in a pink T-shirt, white jeans, and a little baseball cap from the Gap, Robert verged on stereotypical. There was defi-nitely a limpness to his wrist, and he had a dramatic inflection to his voice, the so-called gay accent. But what I noticed most was that he radiated love. He was light where my father was dark. Robert seemed easygoing and comfortable, whereas my dad was weighted down, even suspicious. Robert was just what my father needed. I adored him immediately.

I now wonder if Robert's gaydar went off when he met me; he always joked that he assumed everyone was gay, at least until proven otherwise.

NOT LONG THEREAFTER, MY dad moved into Robert's one-bedroom cottage in San Francisco. I met "the girls," Robert's mother and grandmother, who lived together nearby. Robert often took the two elderly ladies shopping at the grocery store or out to lunch and cocktails at Trader Vic's. They were both growing more dependent, but he never treated them like helpless old biddies. He never forgot that having fun—and I mean adult fun, like a martini and a cigarette—was just as necessary for their well-being as keeping doctors' appointments or taking their medications.

Because Robert had lived in the Bay area since birth, he knew all the interesting spots and could recount a colorful history of the city from memory. Robert made disparate characters and places come alive, amusingly referring to then-mayor Dianne Feinstein as "DiFi" and Sutro Tower, the huge radio antenna that overlooks the Castro, as "the Roach Clip." Robert had come of age in San Francisco in the hedonistic, activist days of the seventies. He had worked against the Briggs Initiative, legislation that would have outlawed lesbian and gay teachers in public schools. He did his share of partying in those days, too: If I told him I was going out hip-hop dancing at the Kennel Club, he could describe the linoleum in the place five clubs back. Robert loved the evolving pageantry of San Francisco. Spurred by his memories, I fell in love with it, too.

Robert was a middle-income manager at the phone company, but he loved to splurge on the people he cared about. His generosity was evident in everything from preparing dinner and margaritas whenever the mood seized him to giving me his faded old 501s. He always seemed to be driving me somewhere average but taking a uniquely lovely route to get there. Fetching me, Alice, and our laundry from our flat in Haight-Ashbury became an excuse to watch the sunset from Twin Peaks; taking me to the airport was a reason to have dinner at the Peppermill in Daly City, a restaurant lit up like Vegas. Robert seemed to have that innate ability to make everyone feel special and loved. Of course, there were times he probably didn't feel much like Glinda the Good Witch, but he didn't like to show that side to the world. If he was feeling angry or annoyed, he preferred to go in his room and close the door.

FIVE YEARS BEFORE ROBERT died, I came out to him and my dad, in the same unspoken way my dad had revealed himself to me. We were on vacation in Lake Tahoe for my birthday (Robert's idea), and I brought along a girlfriend. Dad and Robert could see the stealthy glances that we exchanged as I passed the biscuits on Sunday morning or as we horsed around in the hotel's swimming pool. And that was it. They knew. I never had to say a word. For a long time, I was reticent about telling my mother, who perhaps feared I would "contract" homosexuality from my father like a genetic illness. But Robertoria knew, and his support buoyed me on to greater honesty and visibility about my sexuality.

Over the next few years, I met my girlfriend Alice and became an editor at a gay magazine. Through it all, Robert remained the one older friend who knew me better than my own parents. For example, when I got the job at the magazine, my father's concerns centered on what such a job meant for my career prospects. But Robert was thrilled, and he immediately renewed his subscription. Not only that, he regularly stopped by the magazine's offices, just a few blocks from his job at Pacific Bell, to take me out to lunch. My father still wasn't very happy about my working in gay publishing, but his stance seemed to soften.

SOON AFTER I HAD graduated college, my dad told me that Robert was HIV positive. Robert had found out at about the same time he and my dad had gotten together but had never told me outright. I wasn't really surprised; it was the height of the epidemic in San Francisco, and it seemed like every gay man that age had AIDS. My father assured me that Robert was still perfectly healthy—and that my father himself was negative and would stay that way. He also told me not to tell Robert that I knew; Robert didn't like to talk about it. From that moment I cherished Robert even more, knowing that our time together was limited.

Too soon, Robert's health began to fail. He was often tired, he developed horrible headaches, and he kept a pharmacopoeia of drugs by his bedside. By his last Christmas, he was injecting the drugs directly through a heplock in a vein in his arm. It was terrifying. Every time I left the city, I was afraid that Robert would die while I was away, and I was nervous about the prospect of being so far away once I moved to New York. But the knowledge that he had never been so sick that he had to go to the hospital made me feel a bit better; I figured that I would know when he took a turn and that I could come back to be with him at the end.

I was wrong. Robert developed pneumonia and went quicker than any of us could have known. My father called me the night before Robert died to tell me that he was in the hospital. I frantically called the airlines to arrange a ticket to leave the next morning. When I called my father back, he told me not to bother. Robert died a few hours later.

I was crushed. This death was so incredibly, undeniably unfair. I was angry at my father for not telling me how sick Robert was until it was too late, even though I now realize that Robert didn't want anyone to see him in his last days. After all, where would the Good Witch have been without her wardrobe mistress and perfectly coiffed hair?

NO ONE CALLED UP with gift suggestions for this Father's Day. I still don't have any idea what my dad really wants, besides having Robert back. And that's what we both want. But Robert left us both a gift: he taught us how to be gay. He taught us how to be strong, and stylish, and how to never stop living. He taught us how to be proud of ourselves and how to be kind. As usual, I still don't know what to get for Father's Day. In the meantime, I hope this will do.

THE PLAIN TRUTH

Meema Spadola

The morning my mother moved out, she had the radio tuned to WERU, a community station about an hour up the coast from our small town of Searsmont, Maine. I watched silently as she folded her clothes and stacked books into neat piles around her and my father's bedroom. She went downstairs to make tea, and I sat among her boxes. A song I'd never heard before—a humorous political rallying cry—came on the radio with the lyrics, "Here come the lesbians!" I just sat there, listening, a vague bubble of a thought rising in me. This was the first time I ever heard the word *lesbian*. I was ten years old.

After all her belongings were loaded into her car and my younger brother, Emilio, and I watched her disappear down our long driveway, I found a blank fabric-covered book that my mother had left behind. I started keeping a journal, documenting my life and my parents' separation—in an attempt, perhaps, to somehow control the uncontrollable. Almost twenty years later, I am beginning my thirty-sixth journal, still faithfully documenting.

A few weeks earlier, when my parents told Emilio and me, over Saturday morning pancakes, that they were separating and that my mother would move out, they said only, "We can't live together any more." Of course they loved us, they said, reassuringly. They would never stop loving us. There was no further explanation, even though I promised my bedroom to my mother so that she wouldn't have to leave. Later that day, in a show of familial solidarity, the four of us bundled up to play an early

spring baseball game in the muddy field below our house. As if
nothing had changed.

In the weeks that followed, there were no more discussions
and no more announcements. I didn't ask why my mother was
leaving. If my parents couldn't tell me the truth, then the truth
had to be too horrible to tell. So I became a detective in my
own life. For a while I thought that perhaps my father had
committed a crime. I heard both of my parents' whispered conversations with friends and extended family, the word *lawyer*
mentioned here and there. I jealously monitored my mother's
contact with men. I noted in my journal when a friend's divorced father eyed her. I tried to predict which man in our small
community she'd be most likely to date. I was silent and hostile
toward a male friend of my mother's. "At first I tried to hate
Bill," I wrote in my diary. "You know why. I got upset in the
car, but Mom said she wasn't going to marry him. Good."
Later, years before Bill began wasting away from an AIDS-
related illness, my mother told me that he was gay.

When my mother took me to visit an old friend of hers in
New York City, the friend's daughter, who was my age but so
sophisticated, slyly whispered to me before we left, "I know the
real reason your parents got divorced." A combination of pride
and fear kept me from asking what she knew. I stubbornly continued my own investigation. Every weekend that my brother
and I visited with my mother, I scanned for clues to her new
life but found none that I could decode. She rented a narrow,
bare room in the house of a divorced friend whose children
spent the weekends with their father. She took us to potluck
dinners, attended by women who built log cabins in the woods,
wore flannel shirts, and ate macrobiotic food. Once I went with
my mother to the Susan B. Anthony Club, in an abandoned
nineteenth-century opera house where the women smoked,
danced, and played pool. I was too excited by my night out to
notice there weren't any men there.

Sometime in the year after my mother left, I knew that she
was a lesbian. There is no record of this in my journals, as if I
was too scared to commit the realization to paper. I don't recall
an exact moment that she told me, though years later, my

mother insisted that she had explained to me that her life had changed, that she was "spending time with new people, creating a new circle of friends. A circle of *women* friends." In retrospect, it seems that there was the period of total mystery and then, almost suddenly, the knowledge that my mother was gay. And as soon as I knew the truth—as much as I could understand what it meant for my mother to be a lesbian—I stopped writing about it in my diary, as if ignoring it would make it disappear. The pages were filled instead with long accounts of crushes on boys, alliances and ruptures with other girls, and careful measurements of my slowly developing body.

And yet, in sixth grade, at the back of the school bus, I ventured a whispered confession to my best friend, Andy. He had been my ally since I moved to town in second grade, and I thought that he would understand this, too. But instead of the sympathetic response I expected, he was horrified because my mother—who seemed like such a nice person, after all—was condemned to hell. "Maybe she's not," I quickly retreated, not wanting to repeat the word *lesbian* in front of him. "I meant she's friends with women. I've seen her hug or kiss them on the cheek. Nothing more." We sat quietly for the rest of the ride home, neither one of us sure how to bridge the sudden gap between us.

After this first and only admission, I fiercely guarded my secret. When classmates would come to my mother's apartment during my weekend visits, I "straightened up" the house. I turned any suspicious books—say, *The Joy of Lesbian Sex* or *Nice Jewish Girls: A Lesbian Anthology*—around in the bookshelves so the titles were hidden. I'd hide the framed black-and-white photo of my mother with her arms around her lover. I secreted away the blue handmade pottery lamp with a naked dancing woman; it could be a dead giveaway. After my thirteenth birthday party, I forgot to rearrange the bookshelves back to normal after my friends left, and when my mother asked, I offered only a vague excuse, unable to meet her eyes. She didn't pursue the question, although I'm sure she knew what I was doing.

I wish that there had been some kind of rough guide to life

as the daughter of a divorced lesbian mom living in a rural town, population one thousand. Instead, I learned how to blend in, improvising my way through the years between my parents' separation and the moment that I left home for college and discovered a different world.

In high school I heard the word *queer* so many times that I lost count. On one of our first dates, my first boyfriend—older and cooler—explained the male earring code to me, "Left is okay, but right is wrong." Even though I felt a guilty twinge, I smiled and nodded, so eager to please, knowing then that I'd never tell him about my mother even as I invited him over for a friendly game of Trivial Pursuit with the family.

I lied. I lied so many times it became reflexive. Distant family friends would inquire, "I hear that your father remarried. Is your mother seeing anyone?" I would avoid the truth, afraid of disapproval: "She's too busy working to meet anyone new."

I was constantly reminded that it wasn't safe to tell the truth. One day during my senior year, my mother and I took a Saturday trip to an out-of-the-way rocky beach, where we swam and picnicked and walked by the water, our arms linked. On an empty stretch along the shore, two boys followed us from a cowardly distance, throwing rocks and shouting, "Lezzies!" My mother didn't defend us. She simply gathered our belongings and hurried me back to the car. We rode home without a word, my stomach clenched and anxious.

I turned a corner quite suddenly when I was seventeen, and I left home to attend a small liberal arts college outside of New York City. Even though I was a scholarship student with a limited wardrobe and a notable lack of European vacations, I realized that I could use the "daughter of a lesbian" card to trump my classmates' status symbols. I learned how to subtly drop this into conversation, no matter the topic. New friends and classmates were surprised, though it was uncool to show it, and they recovered quickly, with exclamations of admiration and envy: "That's totally cool," or "You're so lucky." In the straight world at least, I had gained entrée into a minority group.

To some people, being the daughter of a lesbian wasn't just

cool, it was sexually charged, as if my mother's identity made me seem more erotically adventurous. Back at home during the summer after my first year of college, I worked at a documentary production company, the director of which was a friend's father. One weekend, my friend and I were at her family's lake house, floating in inner tubes as her father watched us. "You should do a film about your mother," he told me. "You and your mother. Point the camera at yourself and tell your story. They might not admit it, but people want to know how it affected you. It's sexy." I'd direct. He'd produce and get it on television. I loved the idea of being promoted from production assistant to director, though I was uneasy about the project's so-called sexy factor.

At first my mother was supportive, until I told her that it would include my story, her story. "You have no right to out me," she told me, obviously scared. She was still living in Maine. She feared eviction. She worried that clients might abandon her private therapy practice. And she was afraid of being assaulted. "Gay people get bashed, lesbians are raped, simply because they are lesbians," she told me, on the verge of tears. I was furious. I never had a choice: she changed her life and it changed mine. But my mother looked terrified. I realized that I never knew just how much she feared being out. In deference, I put the documentary aside.

Then, in my last year of college, I started working on *My Mother's Secret*, a do-it-yourself no-budget video about children of lesbians. By then, everything was shifting—she had moved to Boston to go back to school—and like me, getting out of Maine proved to be the route to getting out of the closet. So I didn't ask for my mother's permission; sometime along the way I told her what I was doing, and she offered her cautious approval.

In the film, I chose to tell the stories of five other sons and daughters of various ages whose mothers, like mine, had come out after a divorce. They told virtually identical anecdotes of keeping secrets, lying to friends, and having difficulty understanding their mothers' sexuality. They could have been me.

"How would you define 'lesbian'?" I asked nine-year-old Eben as he squirmed uncomfortably in his chair.

"It's something that happens, and kids don't usually like it happening."

"Do you ever wish you could change it?" I pursued.

"Yes, all the time," he said, glaring straight into the camera. "I just want my family back to normal."

Still, I kept circling around my own story. "I'm unsure of how I want to use myself in the documentary," I wrote in my journal as I began editing the video. "I've expected everyone else to be honest, so what do I say?" In the end, even though my voice-over provided a narrative thread for the video and linked all of the interviews, I remained invisible, using old family photos instead of appearing on camera. Watching the film today, I have the sense that I wasn't as ready to break the habit of secrecy as I had hoped. Instead, I used these people to say the things that were the most difficult for me to express.

Still, there was something powerful about being able to show the finished project to my mother, my anger neatly contained. And instead of being defensive or angry at me, as I feared, my mother loved the documentary. She even came to one of its festival screenings with me.

In the following years, the topic kept resurfacing, and people often asked when I would do a follow-up piece. As I discovered a whole community of gay and lesbian parents, I had this sense that there was a broader story about the experience of their children. As if a whole community's existence was being kept secret. So finally, a decade after I first came to the subject, I returned to it with *Our House: a very real documentary about kids of gay and lesbian parents*. It is sanctioned by my mother and will air on national television. This time I'm not playing narrator; as much as possible, I've let the kids speak for themselves.

But it's just not that simple to dredge up all the old details of the past. I should have known that I couldn't do that without repercussions. During interviews, in person, on the phone, and via e-mail, I repeated my story over and over to nearly three hundred children and parents across the country, until it became a neatly packaged spiel. But then, every once in a while, an interview would turn back on me, and I would be faced yet again with that uncomfortable moment—so reminiscent of high school—of wondering how much to reveal.

So there I was with the realization that despite all those years of documenting in my diaries and my professional life, before I could begin filming, I had to understand more than the mere fact that my mother was a lesbian. I needed to know, finally, about the adult entanglements that lurked beneath the conversation, too complicated to explain to children. Did my mother always know she was gay? Did she love my father? Why did she leave me and my brother? Why couldn't she come out to me? I drew up a list of questions—always the prepared interviewer. My mother, fortunately, was willing; she must have known that we'd need to have this conversation some day. We started slowly, and as we went along we both relaxed, as we found that talking about this wouldn't hurt as much as we feared. When I asked when she knew that she was a lesbian, she said she didn't know. "But you have to understand, Meema," she said. "When I was growing up, the possibility of being gay was like wanting to have two heads. It just didn't occur to me."

When she realized that being a lesbian wasn't an option but rather an imperative, it was terrifying to see my father, me, and my brother on one side, and this new life on the other. "I felt as if I were spanning the Grand Canyon and that I'd fall in and die unless I picked a side. But how could I explain the power of sexual longing to a child?" she wondered aloud. And for the first time, I could sympathize with her—this thirty-four-year-old woman with two small children who must have been so scared. "And so I came out; I'm just sorry that I didn't help you come out, too," she said at last.

Nineteen years after she packed her boxes and left, she was ready to talk. And finally, I was ready to listen.

SHE'LL ALWAYS BE MY DADDY

Laurie Cicotello

When MacGregor and I walked out of the theater after seeing *Back to the Future* on Halloween night, it was pouring rain. I called my dad from the pay phone in the lobby and asked him to come pick us up.

"I can't," he said.

"Why not?" I demanded, unhappy at the thought of walking home in the downpour. I persisted until he finally stammered, "I can't because . . . because I'm dressed as Dana."

"That's okay," I answered, feeling relieved that it was Halloween. "MacGregor will think it's only a costume." After convincing my reluctant father to come get us, I coached MacGregor on what was going to happen. A few minutes later, my dad arrived, dressed in an expensive pink running suit with daisies appliquéd on the front and wearing matching pink tennis shoes.

"Nice costume, Mr. Cicotello," MacGregor said.

I didn't know whether to laugh or cry.

WHAT MY DAD DIDN'T know at the time was that I had already told MacGregor the whole awful truth. As a fourteen-year-old Ms. Pacman junkie, I was always running out of money, and so I had started raiding my house, including my parents' bedroom. One afternoon, as I was rummaging through my dad's nightstand drawer, I found three glossy "she-male" porno magazines. I thought it was kind of weird but rationalized that maybe my dad was just reading them for the articles. Then, farther down in the drawer, I unearthed professional photos of my dad dressed as a woman. My mind began racing, trying to figure out what was going on. *Wait a minute*, I wondered. *Is my dad actually turned on by these magazines?* I shuddered at the thought.

Still, my initial horror didn't keep me from studying those pictures every chance I got during the next few weeks. Then, in a drawer in the small oak credenza in the dining room, I found a small, fat, blue-covered notebook. I started flipping through and reading it. It was my dad's diary, all about his longing to be a woman. He was worried that my mom would leave him and even more terrified of what would happen "if Laurie ever finds out about me." The kicker, though, came toward the end of the book: He actually wrote that he might kill himself if I ever knew. I started bawling like crazy. I couldn't wait to talk to someone. I called MacGregor that afternoon and told him about everything I'd found.

It seems odd to me now that I was able to trust a fourteen-year-old guy with this type of secret, but MacGregor never turned on me. He encouraged me to talk to my Grandma Cicotello—after all, she was my dad's mother, and if anyone could explain what was going on, she could. I mustered the courage to call her and say that we needed to talk. She picked me up in her shiny blue sedan a few hours later and took me back to her house.

We sat in her kitchen, surrounded by her collection of in-struments from the days when she was a professional musician. I was really nervous about admitting to her that I'd been snooping around my parents' things. But I just took a deep breath and said in a rush, "Grandma, I found pictures and a diary of my dad's. Do you know anything about him wearing women's clothes?" Once the words were out, the tears came too. Then I realized Grandma was also crying. She sat very still, her eyes reddening with tears.

"God," she exclaimed. "You weren't supposed to find out!"

"Find out what?" I demanded.

"That your dad wants to be a woman," she said, matter-of-factly. "I knew from the time your dad was very young. Your granddad never knew, or he never said."

After talking and crying for hours, Grandma dabbed at her puffy eyes and looked at me. "Laurie," she said in a slightly shaky voice. "I think it's time we talked to your father." I nodded. The next day, we invited my dad to go miniature golfing, and then we sprung it on him in the parking lot at the Kennedy golf course. Grandma was choked up and could barely talk. My dad was sobbing. I was sniffling into my wad of shredded tissues. Then we went and played the worst round of miniature golf in the history of the world. Miss the windmill, cry. Miss the hole, cry. It was a terrible day.

It was also the capstone of the worst year my dad ever had. He had just been fired from his dream job. He'd spent a great deal of time having lunches with his female coworkers, studying and learning their mannerisms and speech patterns so that he could eventually fit in as a woman. The men in his office, however, saw him as a womanizer and would not sympathize when he was suddenly laid off.

My dad sank into an awful depression and became suicidal. He spent a year in a daze. He tells people now that he was suffering from post-traumatic stress syndrome. It was during this time when I found the pictures and the diary telling how he'd kill himself if I ever found out. When I did find out, I felt as though I'd signed a death warrant on my own father. And in a way I did, because Dan, my *father*, died, and Dana, my *parent*, took his place.

MY FATHER HAD STARTED his transition seven years earlier, in 1978, when he got out of the navy. We moved to Colorado and he started growing his hair long. He also grew his nails long and got his ears pierced. My friends all thought my father was cool because he looked like a rock star. Heck, by then George Michael had his ears pierced, too. It never crossed my mind that my dad looked like a woman. I didn't notice the subtle changes until several years later, when I was poring over photos from that time and thought to myself, "Wow, how could I miss something so obvious?"

I found out later that, during that time, my father had also started electrolysis. Still, I didn't notice any real difference in him. The only change that really confused me were those few times when, as I was watching TV late at night, Dad would come home and act strangely. I clearly remember his shadowy figure in the doorway, saying sternly, "Laurie, go to bed," not offering a hug or a kiss as my dad always did. I can also remember a few times when my mom made me stay in my room with the door closed while my dad left the house. I could hear him putting on his coat and going out the door, and I couldn't understand how he could leave without kissing me first.

My dad traveled all over the world for business, and it seemed like every time my mom and I would drop him off at the airport, some radio station would be playing Elton John's song, "Daniel," which was my dad's name, and I would sing along: *Daniel's traveling tonight on a plane . . . oh, and I can see Daniel waving good-bye . . .* When my dad returned, he would come off the plane full of hugs and kisses and little presents for me, like a Paddington Bear bank and a replica of Lady Diana's engagement ring.

But those mysterious late-night excursions were different—there was such a distance between us. I'm so lucky that nothing ever happened to my father back then, because all those nights, I never had the chance to say good-bye.

THE FIRST TIME I saw Dana in women's clothes, she was standing at the stove, cooking spaghetti in a floral-print romper. I almost started laughing but then ran to my room and cried. It was hard for both my mom and me to accept the person Dana was becoming. For a while, we both found ways to punish her for the changes she was making us go through.

One of the ways my mom and I both got back at Dana was

the "Oops, I left the garage door open again" trick. Dana was petrified at the thought of the neighbors finding out about her, so the garage became her closet. With the garage door closed, Dana could get into the car, start it up, open the garage door with the remote, and safely drive away. The neighbors would never guess who the big woman in the car was, right?

So my mom or I would make some lame excuse for opening the door as Dana was getting ready. Then we'd "forget" to close it, and when Dana left, it was "Hello, world!" Dana would have to make a mad dash for the car. Though she'd yell at us later, we kept "forgetting" for more than three years.

In public, we became adept at blowing pronouns. Today I still slip up sometimes and call Dana "he" or "him," but back then we did it on purpose, to show Dana that we still thought of her as a man, a husband and father, not this strange new woman who wore frilly, fancy sweatsuits and pink lipstick and who spoke in an artificial-sounding falsetto. Every time my mother or I said "he" or "his" in public, Dana would respond with a dirty look, an elbow in the ribs, or a kick under the table. But being corrected in public just made me angrier, and I would keep calling Dana "him."

Often we would tell Dana outright how awful her taste in clothes was. My mom complained often and loudly about Dana's makeup. "Must you wear so much eye shadow when we are only going to the grocery store?" she'd snap. I also adamantly refused to kiss Dana when she was dressed up.

Finally, Dana decided we should start seeing a family therapist to try to deal with our feelings about her transition. I didn't mind the idea; in fact, I was curious to learn more about what was happening with her.

Dana began explaining the differences between being a cross-dresser and being a transsexual on the way over to my first visit to the therapist's office. The therapist, a stocky middle-aged woman with short brown hair, then started in with more education about who my dad really was. There was so much terminology that I was a tad overwhelmed: sex reassignment, transgender, transsexual, transvestite, hermaphrodite, androgyny, male-to-female, female-to-male, homosexuality, bisexuality, asexuality . . . the list went on and on.

Then, the bombshell: The therapist explained that my dad was going to be undergoing a form of puberty, much like my own—except that it was *more* important for his mental health than it was to mine. I was told to expect my dad to borrow my clothes, my makeup, and my jewelry.

This really made me angry. I felt like I was being made a second-class citizen in my own house, like whatever "blooming" was supposed to take place at my age was being put on the back burner. My parents wouldn't let me wear makeup, and all I had was stupid teenager jewelry, but I was determined I wouldn't let my dad wear my clothes! I had already started hoarding food, and now I began eating even more. I packed on weight. I thought that if my dad and I were different sizes, then he couldn't wear my clothes. Slowly, my molehill tummy turned into a mountain belly.

The therapist believed that families shouldn't stay together when one partner comes out as transsexual. My mom and dad didn't agree with her, but they did notice that the transition was having a negative effect on me. My mom had the bright idea to send me to a self-esteem workshop. It cost a hundred dollars for one afternoon. We all had to choose a mantra to repeat over and over. Mine was "I like myself, just the way I am"—fat, greasy-haired, pimply and all. I went to my next session with the therapist and proudly talked all about my self-esteem class. She looked at me and said coldly, "If you don't like yourself the way you are, then why bother saying that you do?" My mom was furious when I told her. She was out a hundred dollars at a time when money was extremely tight in our family, and I didn't want to chant anymore.

STRANGELY ENOUGH, IT WAS a late-night cult movie that started me on the road to accepting Dana for who she was. I first heard of the *Rocky Horror Picture Show* from my friend Jenny, who was the other member of the children of transgendered parents support group I had started. During a sleepover at her house, Jenny played the soundtrack for me and I was hooked. I really wanted to see the movie, but I didn't have the courage to go alone. Luckily, my friend Rory had made the foray several times, and agreed to take me. We picked up his girlfriend, and the three of us headed for the theater, blasting the soundtrack all the way there.

I was amazed at what—or how little—people wore. There were men dressed as women, wearing corsets, fishnets, and sexy underwear like Frank N. Furter from the movie. There were other people, both men and women, dressed as characters like Riff Raff, with shaved heads and gold vests, and Magenta, the maid, in mini-skirted uniforms. Even the people who weren't dressed up looked totally strange to me in their leather motorcycle jackets, spiked hair dyed blue and purple, pierced noses, and thick combat boots. As I talked to people before the show, I told them that my dad was transgendered. I felt surprisingly comfortable telling these complete strangers my family secret, and they gave me instant acceptance, even admiration. A tall, lanky man with shaggy blond hair and a dazed look in his eyes said, "Your dad is transsexual? That's so cool!" He introduced himself as "Roger the Paranoid Schizophrenic Bisexual." We sat together, and toward the end of the show he leaned over and kissed me on the mouth. It was my first kiss ever. I left the show completely ecstatic.

I would return every week for months, sometimes with Rory, sometimes alone. *Rocky Horror* opened my mind and liberated me sexually. It helped me to begin accepting my dad, as well as other people who don't fit the "normal" mold.

But complete acceptance didn't come until after I went away to a small liberal arts college in Nebraska. In my first semester there, Siobhan Tyler, a girl in my dorm, confided that she'd been an incest victim and that her father was now in jail for abusing her. When I told Siobhan about Dana she suggested that I keep quiet about it; Siobhan kept quiet about her past, rather than risk certain humiliation. But word travels fast in a small college community, and pretty soon most of the other students knew about Siobhan, despite her efforts to preserve her secret. She got a reputation for being "loose" with the male students, and people began to make fun of her behind her back and tease her to her face. She would find condoms left in her mailbox and pamphlets about venereal diseases taped to her door. Seeing how Siobhan was harassed was all I needed to convince me to come forward and loudly admit who my dad was. I told anyone who would listen about *Rocky Horror* and about my transgender parent. I was called into the dean of students' office and told that they had received complaints that I was talking about sex too much. But that didn't stop me. I helped to organize and start a group on campus called the Peer HIV Education Organization. It was then OK to talk about sex on campus, as long as we talked about safer sex at the same time.

What was really cool, though, was overhearing kids around campus talk about me in an accepting way. Someone would whisper as I walked past, "Hey, did you hear that her dad is a transsexual?" And I would smile when the other party would casually respond, "Yeah, so?"

IT WAS HARDER FOR other members of my family to fully accept my father as a woman. When my mom's mom, Grandma Goeden, was visiting several years ago, my parents expected me to tell her about Dana. We spent the afternoon watching television while I waited for the perfect opportunity. I had only a small window of time before Dana got home from work in a lovely print dress, hose, and heels, and that window was shrinking quickly.

Finally I turned the volume down and told Grandma that we needed to talk. I told her that I had to tell her something about Dana. I wanted to make the explanation as easy for Grandma as I could. I started by asking her if she'd seen any talk shows about men who wanted to be women. She nodded.

I asked if she knew anyone who was like that. She didn't. I asked if she'd noticed anything unusual about my dad. No again. So I told her that Dana was like one of the people on the talk shows, that Dana wanted to be a woman.

"Grandma," I said nervously. "My dad is like some of the people you've seen on talk shows. But she is not all wild and crazy like the transsexuals on those shows."

Grandma's eyes glazed over. "I think the weather will be staying warm for a few days," she said.

"Grandma, did you hear me?" I asked.

"Unless the weather turns cold," she said.

Eventually, I gave up. She just wasn't willing to listen. When Dana came home, Grandma stared in disbelief. My father didn't say anything and went to change her clothes.

I don't know what Grandma would have said if I'd told her that Dana and my mom actually *were* on one of those talk shows. They were invited to be guests on *Jenny Jones* back in 1992. My mom wasn't even going to go in the first place, but Dana convinced her that it would be good for their relationship and would help raise awareness. A limousine picked them up and flew them to Chicago for filming. My mom wore a blond wig and had her voice disguised.

Dana, who viewed the show as a serious opportunity to educate people, ended up coming off as too stiff and technical, while the other transgender couples that were guests obviously thought the whole thing was a hoot. When Jenny announced that a transgender woman and her female partner would be getting married on the show, the other guests cheered and went off to change into matching bridesmaid dresses. My parents hadn't gotten to Chicago early enough to be fitted for bridesmaid ensembles, so they just sat there looking uncomfortable.

I ended up watching the show in the basement of my dorm, surrounded by about thirty of my dorm mates! The worst part was when Jenny asked my mom about her and Dana's sex life. My mom stumbled and stammered through her answer: "Well, sex is not that important to me. What's important is . . . um . . . having a best friend who can, um . . . fix my car and, um, kill spiders for me. . . ."

I spent hours after the show answering questions about Dana. But by then I was comfortable about it. The most common question, of course, was if she had had the surgery. I told them the truth—that, although I know Dana takes female hor-

mones supplemented with Evanesce and Feminol (herbal estrogen enhancers), I don't know if she has had the surgery. I made
the decision long ago that I did not care to know one way or
the other about what equipment Dana had or has. Besides,
knowing would not make any difference as to how I feel about
her as my parent.

IT WASN'T UNTIL A few years after they appeared on *Jenny
Jones* that my mom truly accepted Dana. In 1997, after Colorado Republican state senator Marilyn Musgrave introduced an
anti–same-sex marriage bill into the Colorado State Legislature,
Dana testified to the legislature on numerous occasions about
the dangers of passing the bill, which would require the disso-
lution of my parents' marriage. During this time, Senator Musgrave was quoted in the *Denver Post* as saying, "Children are
better off raised in traditional families." I could not stomach
this thought and dashed off a letter to the *Post*, which started,
"As the proud Republican daughter of a transgender parent, I
have to disagree with Marilyn Musgrave. I was much better off
raised in a nontraditional family."

My mom just about had a heart attack when my letter was
printed with my real name at the bottom. She didn't want everyone at her office to know whom she was married to. I tried to
explain to her what I had learned at college, that by coming out
to everyone herself, she took away the power of her coworkers
to make fun of her. I told her that any cruel jokes that might
come up could be answered with a simple: "Yeah? So?" She
didn't believe me at the time, but over the years, she has come
to see that it's true.

After my letter was published, I accompanied Dana the next
time she testified. After being harshly criticized in the testimony,
Senator Musgrave went out into the hallway with a staffer. No
one else would talk to her, so I went up and introduced myself.
She shook my hand for a very long time. I think she believed
me to be her only friend in the room. Then I asked if she'd read
my letter. The color drained from her face, and she snapped her
hand away, spitting out, "I read it!" Then she walked away.

The anti-same-sex marriage bill was vetoed twice by then-governor Roy Romer (Democrat), due in part to Dana's testimony. At the time of this writing, in 1999, the new Colorado governor, conservative Republican Bill Owens, has promised to sign the bill into law if it ever reaches his desk. But Dana is committed to making sure that doesn't happen. Since testifying, Dana has become a public speaker who teaches male-female communication and interaction. She has even become an annual speaker at one Denver high school. And she and my mother remain legally married after thirty-one years.

Shortly after my letter was published in the *Post*, Dana was invited to be a speaker at the 1997 Denver PrideFest Rally. My mom and I accompanied Dana to the podium in front of fifty-five thousand people. This was a far cry from *Jenny Jones* in 1992, and I was proud that my mom was able to stand there without her wig and voice distorter—even if she was still a bit annoyed about being pushed so abruptly out of the closet. Dana spoke movingly about the importance of keeping families together. At the end of her speech, Dana took my mom's hand and mine and raised them, telling the cheering crowd: "Colorado Springs, I've got your family values, right here!"

TAMBOURINE DANCER

Rivka Solomon

Busy tonight, Rivka?" Mom asked as she gathered up a half dozen economy-size bags of generic potato chips in her arms. That was just like her, trying to grab hold of as much as she could.

"No," I answered hesitantly, picking up the two bags she dropped. I still couldn't believe that here I was, fifteen years old, and I'd ended up with nothing to do on a Saturday night. In my high school, in 1978, only the dorks were Saturday-night-stay-at-homers.

"Like to help at a fund-raiser for the theater? It's a women's party," my mom said. My parents' theater was always broke, but they didn't care; they could always throw another party to help pay for the bills for one more week.

I remembered the one other all-women's party I'd been to a year earlier, when I was fourteen. I'd gone with my mom that night only because my friends were going to see *Jaws* and I'd already seen it twice. But I ended up having a good time. Carol, an old family friend, was a rich doctor. She and her girlfriend of ten years had rented a yacht in Boston Harbor. Outrageous decorations, excellent food, loud music; it must have cost a mint. Most of the party goers were lesbians. There were as many women in tuxes as there were in fancy dresses. At first I couldn't help but stare. But by the end of the night it was nothing special. Just a bunch of boring adults—like always.

Thinking back to the good grub and loud music of the yacht

party, I told my mom, "Okay. But I don't care if it's a fund-raiser, you better pay minimum wage or I'll be an exploited worker."

"Ten bucks. But you can invite a friend if you want."

"Naw, that's okay." Was she crazy? My friends weren't ready for women in tuxes. It was only a few months ago in junior high when kids were calling girls "lezzies" for acting weird—or for nothing at all.

I threw on a T-shirt and jeans and jumped in the car.

By midnight, my work for the night—collecting the cover charge at the door and filling plastic cups full of wine—was over. The place was packed. If there was a building fire code, we had long since violated it. The living room floor was creak-ing and dangerously rocking as more than one hundred women bounced up and down in time with the music. I saw a rare open seat on the sofa and grabbed it. I wasn't interested in joining the revelry on the dance floor. The party goers were adults, too old for me to play with.

A stocky, almost chubby, woman sat down on the arm of the couch right next to me. She was younger than many of the others but still older than I was by about a decade. She had on cowboy boots and a leather vest.

She tapped her sternum and yelled over the music, "Cheri."

I nodded. I didn't feel like talking "Rivka."

"You live around here?" Cheri asked as she played with the tassel on her boots.

"Sorta. A fifteen-minute drive."

"Need a ride home?" She grinned.

I shifted around in my seat. I was never comfortable when a guy hit on me, and now I saw it wasn't much easier when the pursuer was female.

"That's okay. I'll get a ride home with my mom." I pointed to the woman in the black sequined jacket who was banging a tambourine above her head as she danced in the middle of a circle of women.

"That's your *mom*!" Cheri gasped, and pointed.

I understood; Mom looked and acted too young to be my

mother. I seemed too old to be her daughter. She was playful exuberance; I was stoic maturity.

"How old are you?" Cheri asked, skeptical.

"Fifteen," I said, hoping it would quash all thoughts of romance.

"Well, I'll be—"

"I'm gonna help with cleanup now. Bye," I said, bolting. Cheri was still watching my mom dance.

BEHIND MY HOUSE—THE house ten commune members called home—there was a tepee my mom had built.

"Come on! Where else can we go?" My new boyfriend nudged.

"I don't think so." Jonathan was my first boyfriend, ever.

"Come on . . ." He took my hand and pulled. The rest of me reluctantly followed. I didn't know what would happen if I went with him into the teepee. And I didn't know if I wanted to know.

I was pulled all the way to the canvas door. Jonathan pushed it aside as I stood at the entrance. He held the green cloth flap open as our eyes adjusted to the darkness inside. Then I saw what looked like movement.

"Oh! Mom! Sorry!"

"Oh. Rivka. No, that's okay . . . uh, Cheri, you remember Rivka."

"Um . . . yeah. Hi, Rivka."

"Uh, hi. Um, this is Jonathan. . . . Okay. Bye." I could have died.

"What was that? That was your *mom*?" Jonathan asked when we were almost out of earshot. He was rushing behind me, trying to catch up. "Who was the other one?"

"Cheri."

"Cheri? Who's she? What were they doing?"

"I don't know."

"You don't know?"

"Let's go inside the house."

"Hey, is your mom a, you know, a *lesbian?*"

"Cheri's just a friend."

"Your mom does it with women? Awesome. . . . Hey, if she's out here, can we go in your bedroom?"

IT WAS AWFUL. AWFUL. I had seen them together. On the floor of the big green tepee, legs entwined. The tepee, where you went only if you didn't want to be bothered, if you wanted to be *alone*. Even if it had been a man I would have hated it. But it wasn't a man, it was a woman. So, what did that mean? I didn't know, and anyway, it didn't really matter much *who*, just that it wasn't Dad.

It was all so confusing, especially because Jonathan had wanted to do just that something with *me*. It was all around me, this sex thing, and I wanted nothing to do with it. At least they'd still had their clothes on.

CHERI'S PRESENCE IN MY mom's life soon became a constant. She wasn't half bad, really, giving gift after gift of cuddly stuffed animals until there was no more room left on my mom's bed. But I never forgave Cheri. *How dare she . . .* hitting on both daughter and mother on the same night! I carried this resentment with me into all my interactions, all my conversations with her. I also felt funny that Cheri was so young—closer to my age than my mother's.

Looking back now as an adult myself, I wonder why it was these things that bothered me and not that my mom was having an affair with a *woman*. But somehow that hadn't fazed me. Perhaps I had seen too many gay couples at my parents' theater and in their plays to be shocked. The theater was where my parents worked for social change, producing plays about sexism, women's liberation, and male-female relations. And, in the mid-seventies, they did yet another innovative play: In one scene a woman brushed another's hair, gently, tenderly. So tenderly you got ideas. Then, just before the lights dimmed, they kissed.

Men, too—one scene ended with two men rocking each other in a tight embrace.

So I was used to the idea that two men or two women could be together. The shock was that my parents were separating. They were a pair, and the theater was their lifework. But now, even before Cheri entered our lives, my parents had been sleeping in separate rooms for more than half a year, and Mom was planning to move out completely in just a few months' time, before the end of school. She would be on her own and could live her life as she pleased; we all recognized that now. And Cheri's presence didn't seem to bother my father so much either. Maybe he just saw it as my mom experimenting—I don't know, I never asked. Mostly though, I think that (like me) my father was too preoccupied, too devastated, over his wife's leaving— that his world had turned upside down—to care whom Mom happened to be snuggling with.

MY SISTER LEFT HOME at seventeen, soon after my parents separated. She had been itching to get out for years. Communal living was not for her. Or me, but she had finished high school; I had two years to go. Tally always complained loudly, "Why can't I just have a *normal* family?" We were anything but. With the other theater performers, Mom and Dad dressed up like bizarre creatures and performed in front of strangers, even on the streets. They smoked pot occasionally and sometimes experimented with other drugs. And now one of them was having sex with her own kind. Tally was mortified. She never told anyone about Mom becoming a lesbian.

I was different. It didn't bother me. Not now that I was almost through with my sophomore year of high school. Not now that I had my own group of close friends—most of whom were as weird as my parents. We were 70s teen hippies; the alternative kids at the high school. We wore long skirts with hiking boots or torn jeans with huge psychedelic patches. We smoked reefer during lunch. We led loud protests against nuclear power. Everyone at school hated us, especially the jocks, who threw stones and spit when we walked by. But we were comfortable with each other. All my friends knew my mom was warm, open to kids hanging out in her home—and gay.

I never directly discussed my mother's sexual orientation with my friends but never hid it either. No one reacted with shock when they found out. Not that any of *us* were gay. No, we were all safely in heterosexual relationships—or else quiet about our desires. Anyone who wasn't straight waited until years after high school to come out. That is, everyone except my new best friend, June.

"My friends at the Women's Center call me *baby dyke*," she told me with obvious pride when I first met her in eleventh grade. She was the only person in our whole high school who knew more about women's issues than I did. We had too much common knowledge not to become best friends.

But even with June, who felt safe enough to tell me she liked me *that way*, the topic of my lesbian mom rarely surfaced. It was something that was accepted but never discussed: in short, the same arrangement I had with my own mother.

WHEN CHERI WAS OUT, Leonard was in. And there wasn't much time in between. Leonard made Cheri seem good. Heavy lids, a constantly averted gaze, and words that eased slowly, tentatively from his mouth all made me want to shake him and yell *"Anybody home?"* I had acted pissy toward Cheri, but I barely tolerated Leonard. It didn't matter, though, because soon enough he was gone. Jim turned up in his place. Then Diana.

Okay, so my mother was exploring relationships with both men and women. Always, still, trying to embrace as much as she could.

But none of this was my concern. I was now sixteen, smack dab in the dizzying middle of my own teenage whirlwind. Too busy to pay attention to my mother's love dramas. Men, women, what did I care? I had my own issues, like, I don't want to do it, but Jonathan and I are so close to doing it, so should I get fitted for a diaphragm anyway?

Like the topic of my mom's sexuality, I never discussed these confusing things with anyone.

WHEN I SURFACED FROM my teen years and reached, gasping, the oxygen of my early twenties, it was the mid-1980s and the annual gay marches were just beginning to take hold in the Northeast. At the rainbow-balloon-filled march, about one thousand people in my small college town in western Massachusetts chanted and danced. I nodded my head in understanding when I heard the theme was *pride*. The sting of junior high school jabs like *lezzie* had taken its toll on all of us, leaving black-and-blue marks on some in its wake. Pride was the correct—the direct—contradiction.

I went to the march to support June and all the lesbians and the gay men of the world. Though I identified as straight, *We're here. We're queer. Get used to it!* happily skipped out of my mouth with the rest of them. "Another gay teacher," sported one woman's sign. "We are your doctors," said a second. But when I saw the one that said, "Proud mother of a lesbian daughter," then I knew what I had to do.

When I was a teen, being gay, lesbian, or bisexual had been readily accepted in my family environment and at the theater. Perhaps this was why it wasn't until the pride march that I stopped to think about how challenging life must have been for the lesbian closest to me—the lesbian I called Mom. By now, she only dated women, and she was a bold woman, *out* in our suburban town, in her work, in her life. I suddenly wanted to support her just like I'd support any other person dedicated to a struggle for liberation. But although she regularly used the words and spoke the lingo, *I* had never actually done so with her. What should I say? How should I say it?

When it came time for my next visit home I knew I needed to say the words. They were right and true, even if they felt awkward. We were sitting in the yard and talking as my mother pulled huge clumps of tall grass from an overgrown flower bed. We talked about this and that, but the most important words, the ones I wanted to say badly, still didn't come.

Certainly I was proud of my mom. She was strong, smart, and bold—a dynamic tambourine dancer in a circle of women.

"Mom, I'm proud you are a lesbian," I finally blurted out without breathing. It was the only way. "And proud to be your daughter."

"Thanks, Rivka." She smiled, glanced up from her weeding, and said, "Pass me that bucket of mulch, will ya?"

Big whoop. She didn't seem to care much, she was so comfortable with herself and her choices. That's when I wondered, had I said it for her, or had I said it for me? Either way, every Gay Pride march since then I've been sporting my own sign: *Yet Another Daughter Proud of Her Lesbian Mom!*

CHARLOTTE

Meagan Rosser

I need to take some time off from work, Chauncey."

My boss puts down the case files she was reading with an exasperated snort. "You know we're totally short staffed, Meagan. Now is *not* the time to be taking a vacation."

"It's not vacation," I answer, feeling the lump in my throat grow even bigger. "My . . . my mom's . . . someone's sick, she has cancer, and I need to go to Florida and see her."

"Your mother is sick?" Chauncey frowns.

"No!" I say, feeling frustrated. How can I make her understand? "It's not my mom, it's her partner, Charlotte. They just found the cancer, and it's really advanced. I really need to go to Florida." I can feel that my voice is about to break, but I know Chauncey will respect me more if I stay professional, so I take a deep breath and continue. "I've talked to other staff and they'll cover my clients. I'll take the time unpaid if you want. I just really need to go."

I can't tell if Chauncey is annoyed or confused. "I don't know how I feel about this, Meagan," she finally replies, shuffling through the unwieldy pile of papers on her desk. "I mean, maybe if it was one of your *parents* . . ."

At that point, I can't hold back the tears any longer. "She *is* one of my parents," I blurt, barely able to get the words out between sobs. Chauncey just sighs impatiently and hands me a box of scratchy institutional tissues. After a few minutes of cold, awkward silence, I realize that she isn't going to say anything else. "All right," I declare, standing up. "I guess today is

my last day here. I'm going to say good-bye to the clients and
go home."

"For Christ's sake, Meagan," Chauncey stammers, obviously picturing complete bedlam in the psychiatric treatment
center where I have worked for several years. "You don't have
to be so hasty about all of this. I guess we can work something
out."

TWO DAYS LATER, I'M on a plane headed to Florida, where one
of the women who raised me since I was seven is lying in the
hospital, her body consumed by cancer cells that were only discovered during a routine surgery a few days earlier—too late
for the doctors to do anything but give time limits: three, six
months at the most. I am still in shock from hearing Mom's
voice on the phone, and the confrontation with my boss only
made the situation seem more terrifyingly surreal.

As long as I can remember, I've been fielding questions
about who Charlotte is and why she lived with my mom, my
sister, and me. Mom and Charlotte made it clear to us that they
could lose their jobs if the wrong people found out the truth
about them. My elementary school friends swallowed the story
that she was my mom's best friend who had moved in after the
divorce so that they could both save money—especially since I
could point to the guest room closet where Charlotte kept her
clothes and tell them this was her bedroom. But as I got older,
my friends began to ask why I was worried about getting busted
by Charlotte if I stayed out late. "She's not your mom, girl,"
they'd tease. And when my mom got a new job, and we were
getting ready to move from Virginia to South Carolina, my
friends just assumed Charlotte wouldn't be coming. I ended up
telling a few of them the truth. Most of them handled it well,
accepting my mom and Charlotte while still making the same
jokes about "fags" and "dykes" that they always did.

"CHECK OUT THOSE FUDGE packers, man!" Perry yelled, sling-
ing his arm around my shoulder as we walked out the back

door of the high school. With his other arm, he gestured toward a group of boys sitting on the side of the steps, leaning intently over chessboards. I didn't say anything, and smiled nervously. I had never had a serious boyfriend before Perry, and I knew I was in love with him. Perry liked to drive fast, drink Jack Daniel's, and shoot deer. No one could think I was a lesbo while I was with Perry.

After we had been dating for a few months, Perry began to ask me the usual questions about my family: *Who is Charlotte? Why does she act like she's your mother?* I gave him the usual story about my mom and Charlotte just being close friends but he didn't seem to swallow it. "There's something different about your folks," he kept saying. So finally I decided to tell him the truth about my family, after making him swear to God not to tell anyone. We were sitting in his beat-up red Ford Escort parked out in the woods near his house. I turned to him and said nervously, "Perry, I need to tell you something."

I told him, and at first he didn't seem to quite understand. He said, "God that's weird. I mean, I can see why Charlotte would be a lesbian, she practically looks like a man . . . but your mom is really pretty. I bet a lot of guys would be interested in her."

That was true. Mom sometimes talked with bitter amusement about men who were hitting on her. Just two years earlier, my eighth-grade shop teacher had spent weeks questioning me about my mom, especially about whether or not she "was seeing anyone." I was both embarrassed and annoyed. I was half tempted to tell him the truth just to see the look on his face, but I knew Mom would kill me. I thought how funny it was that so many of my friends had no problem seeing Charlotte as a lesbian, but they couldn't believe that my fashion-conscious, lipstick-wearing PTA-president mom could possibly be one, too.

"You know, Perry," I said. "Mom and Charlotte don't want to sleep with men. That is what it means to be a lesbian, after all."

Perry suddenly seemed really disturbed and defensive. "How could your mom be a lesbian if she married your dad and had kids?" he demanded.

"Well," I replied, repeating what my mom had told me when I asked her the same question. "She got married pretty young and didn't realize till she was older that she was just repressing her true feelings."

Perry looked even more alarmed. "You're not repressing anything, are you?" he stuttered.

I could have died. One of my worst fears had always been that people would think that I was a lesbian just because of my mother. I began to get especially panicked, remembering the times I had taken some of Mom and Charlotte's lesbian-themed books out of their closet (yes, that is literally where they were kept) and had read them with disgust and urgent curiosity. "Oh God, no," I said loudly. "I mean, they can do whatever they want, but I would be so grossed out!"

Perry seemed convinced by this answer, but he still wanted to talk about my mom. The next week, after he pulled the car to a stop and turned off the ignition, he reached down under the black Naugahyde seat and pulled out some tattered, colorful-looking magazines. "Look," he said, flipping the top one open. "I wonder if this is what your mom and her girlfriend do. I bet Charlotte is the man. I bet she eats your mom's pussy."

I thought I was going to be sick to my stomach. I understood that Mom and Charlotte were partners and lovers, but no one wants to think about their parents actually having sex. "Put those away!" I shrieked. "I don't want to see that!" Perry laughed and kept showing me the pictures, leaning close and whispering in my ear until I really did think I was going to throw up. But I put up with it, because I was still terrified that he might think I had a personal reason for caring about the picture, that my mom's gayness had somehow rubbed off on me.

AS MY PLANE HITS the runway in Gainesville, I am more scared than I've ever been in my life. For a moment, I'm not even sure I can stand up and walk down the narrow aisle to the exit. "This won't work," I tell myself. "You need to stay strong for Charlotte." Somehow, I manage to get off the plane and take a cab to the hospital. The driver calls me "Honey." His thick Southern accent is comforting and familiar.

I can hear uproarious laughter all the way down the hall to Charlotte's hospital room. When I get to the doorway, I see the backs of two women sitting in chairs drawn up by the bed. They have that familiar white middle-class lesbian look: bilevel haircuts, no makeup, tailored pants, comfortable shoes. Charlotte is propped up on pillows, showing them something in her lap. As I get closer, I see that it's a get-well card signed by her students from the middle school. Charlotte looks up and sees me standing uncertainly in the doorway. She has lost a lot of weight. Her cheeks are sunken, and the circles under her eyes have darkened to a rich plum color. But her eyes and smile have not changed. "Meagan," she calls out in her warm, deep voice. "Barbara, Denise, this is Meagan, my oldest daughter!"

I lose track of the number of women who come to visit Charlotte in the hospital that day. Knowing Charlotte, it doesn't surprise me that she has already made friends in the few weeks she and Mom have lived in Gainesville, but I am amazed that some of her visitors are women she has never even met. Ruby and Lee, two other professors at the university, introduce themselves to Charlotte and me for the first time and then offer to help unpack boxes at the new house and run errands. I thank them for their generosity and Ruby replies, "Oh it's all right, honey. Last year one of us was in the hospital and everyone just got together to help her out."

Later that night, during Barbara and Denise's second visit, they go out to find a ladies' room, and come back looking amused. Barbara nudges Charlotte and says, "I think your night nurse sings for the choir." We all giggle, and the older women talk about various other people around town who might "bat for the team" or "go to their church." When Charlotte starts speaking less and closes her eyes for a few minutes, Denise stands up and touches me on the arm. "Come on, Meagan," she says cheerfully. "I'll give you a ride back to the house, and we can stop on the way for some dinner."

Over heaping plates of genuine Southern barbecue, I confess to Denise how worried I am about Mom. She has never been single in her entire adult life, and it is really hard for me to imagine her without Charlotte. "Don't worry, honey, we'll all make sure they both get taken care of," Denise tells me in her soothing drawl. It is the first time that I've ever been in Gainesville, but I feel nearly at home.

ONE FRIDAY AFTERNOON, DURING my sophomore year in college, I stood in my dorm room getting ready to go to my first Lesbian/Bisexual Women's Union potluck. Four years after breaking up with Perry, I was finally ready to explore those little crushes I'd always had on my best girlfriends. I put on an Indigo Girls T-shirt, a black leather jacket, and Doc Martens boots. "Do I look okay?" I asked my friend Margot, nervously.

"You look fine," she answered impatiently. "Let's go!"

I was still feeling nervous as we walked into the shabby third-floor apartment where the potluck was held. A song by Ani DiFranco was playing, and other people had stacked up their folk music and grrrl rock beside the stereo for later in the night. We all sat around the living room and talked about the patriarchy, who was getting together with whom, and the politics of bisexuality in the women's community. Suddenly I started laughing. Margot asked me why, and I blushed and said, "Oh, never mind, it's kind of hard to explain."

I was remembering the first women's potluck that Mom and Charlotte had at our house. It was about a year after Charlotte had moved in with us, and I still hadn't completely adjusted to my mother and father being divorced. My sister and I were in the TV room, giggling about how weird Mom and her new friends were. There was a group of about ten women sitting in the living room. Most of them seemed to have more hair on their legs than they did on their heads, and they were talking about the patriarchy, who was getting together with whom, and their fears that Ronald Reagan might actually get elected. They listened to "womyn's music" all evening, and I wished that they would change the record. Holly Near's music was awfully depressing. I mean, what eight year old wants to hear a song about people getting killed in Central America?

Suddenly, it occurred to me that I didn't have to keep silent about what I was thinking. In fact, some of the articles and books that we had been assigned as homework reading for my women's studies class had been written by those women from Mom and Charlotte's living room. So I told Margot all about my mom, and she just looked impressed and said, "Wow, what a trip."

MOM AND CHARLOTTE'S NEW house in Gainesville seems tiny compared to the big houses we'd had in Virginia and South Carolina. The walls are flat white, and there are no pictures up yet. There are boxes everywhere, some standing open to reveal stacks of thick books with solid academic bindings. Mom is out of town on a speaking engagement she couldn't manage to cancel. On the refrigerator, I find a list headed "Things for Meagan to do for Charlotte when she comes home from hospital." I take it down and sit at the polished oak table to read it: *Lift boxes. Feed Tiger. Clean bathroom. Cook meals. Go to drugstore. Love, Mom.*

Although I try to relax and watch some TV, I can't stop thinking about how thin Charlotte has gotten, how small she looked in her hospital bed. I really want to talk to someone. I think about my mother's mother, how she always made me feel comforted and safe, telling me, "I love you sixty million barrels," whenever she tucked me into bed. I pick up the phone and dial her house in South Carolina. No answer. She must be out playing bridge with "the ladies." I flip aimlessly through some magazines and then try to call some of my friends in Boston. No one is home. Finally, I pick up the phone and dial my Grandmother Rosser, my dad's mother.

She picks up on the first ring, announcing "Hello," in her thin, regal tones. I can picture her sitting upright, her head tilted like a bird's, on her Malaysian teak chair with the velvet seat, amid her collection of antique Chinese snuff bottles that she acquired on trips around the world. As a little kid, I was always afraid to touch anything in her house, which still feels like a museum. She is thrilled to hear from me and immediately launches into a long story about some tiny wooden sculptures she brought back from a recent trip to Chile. I keep waiting for the right moment to talk to her about Charlotte, but it never comes. "How does your mother like her new house?" she asks at one point, and I say "Fine, but . . . ," and then she's off again.

I hang up thinking *I shouldn't have expected anything different.* Grandmother has always had a way of presenting a carefully selected version of reality to herself and others. Even after my parents divorced and Mom was with Charlotte, Grandmother Rosser kept Mom and Dad's wedding pictures up around her house. She didn't take them down until she could replace them with pictures of my dad and his new wife. Once, when I was about seven and my sister, Caitie, was three, Grandmother dressed Caitie up in the same white lacy family heirloom christening dress that I had seen on myself and my cousins in some of our baby pictures and had asked me to hold her on my lap so that she could take pictures. I told Mom about it when I got home, and she just shook her head and laughed.

"What's so funny?" I asked her.

"Meagan, a christening dress is meant to be worn by a baby at a special ceremony that initiates them into a Christian church. You and Caitie have never *been* christened, but your grandmother probably shows those pictures to her friends so she can pretend that you were."

By now, I have grown to understand that there are certain aspects of life that Grandmother simply refuses to acknowledge. Although Grandmother often asks, "How is your mother doing?" I have never had the gumption to say, "Which one?" She has never said Charlotte's name in my presence, and I hadn't realized how much it bothered me until now.

ONE AFTERNOON BEFORE DINNER, the summer after my sophomore year of college, I found Mom in the master bedroom, pacing around and muttering, "Where the hell is that other damn earring?" Charlotte was sitting on the edge of the bed, looking kind of tense. I was surprised. Usually getting dressed up to go out somewhere with Charlotte put Mom in a good mood.

"Where are y'all going?" I asked.

Mom rolled her eyes and snapped, "I have to go to this stupid party at the university president's house." She put one hand on my shoulder to steady herself while she stepped into her high-heeled black alligator pumps. I was amused to see that Charlotte was still in jeans and a T-shirt; I hated dressing up, too. I turned to her and said, "I guess you're going pretty casual, huh?" and wondered why they both became suddenly quiet.

"Actually," Mom said evenly, "Charlotte isn't coming to the party. I'm going with Fred." Fred was a friend of my parents', a gay man who, like my mom, held a high position at the university and was ambitious to climb the academic ladder even higher. The two of them had decided to go to the party together to cover for each other. Having spent the past two years on my very progressive college campus, I was almost shocked to realize that Mom and Charlotte were still having to hide who they were and make up elaborate stories like the ones I used to tell my childhood friends.

I sat down on the bed and said, "I'm sorry, Mom, it really sucks that you have to do that."

Charlotte put her hand on Mom's shoulder and said, "Honey, I'd better help you look for that other earring. If Fred is better dressed than you are, they'll all know that he's gay, and it'll blow your cover." We all cracked up, and the tension dissolved.

That summer, I felt like I finally understood how hard it had been for Mom and Charlotte to always have to keep their secret while raising us in such a conservative environment. I remembered how angry I was when, during high school, they expressed concern that I was dating an African-American boy. I expected that a lot of the people at school would have a problem with me dating Joseph, but I never thought my ultraliberal parents would possibly side with that gang of girls who cornered me after school and slammed me against the brick wall of the school, scratching my face, pulling my hair, and hissing, "White bitch ho-bag!"

"You're so racist," I wailed at my parents, after they told me that it wasn't a good idea to hold hands with Joseph in the school hallway.

Mom and Charlotte gave each other a knowing, exasperated look. Then Mom said quietly, "Don't you get it, Meagan? We don't care that he's black. But you are bucking the system, and anytime you choose to do that, there are always consequences. That's exactly how it is for Charlotte and me. We're proud of who we are, but we know what we could face if certain people found out. We always have to be careful."

"I can't believe you have the nerve to compare my situation to yours. I mean, at least I'm dating a guy!" I spit back, and stormed out of the room.

No, I didn't get it, and it would be several years before I did. I felt like such a freak back then—when people weren't beating me up for dating a black boy, they were making fun of my hair, my clothes, my bust size—and having lesbian moms was just another thing that made me feel like I must have come from another planet.

A few days before graduating from high school, my friends and I each put some of our parents' liquor into half-empty Coke bottles and got together for a little good-bye party. As we dished the dirt about who was sleeping with whom, I noticed that my friend Dolores was quiet and staring into space. Then she said she needed some air and went outside. Concerned, I followed. I found Dolores pacing around the backyard crying. "What's wrong, girl?" I asked, following in her footsteps as she moved restlessly around the wide square of grass.

"It's nothing, Meagan. Go back inside."

"No. I'm going to follow you around until you tell me what's wrong," I replied, partly because I was buzzed from the mixture of Jack Daniel's and warm Coke sloshing around in my gut. She turned around and looked at me with a little of the old, mischievous Dolores in her eyes.

"I guess you probably will," she said. "You always were a real freakazoid."

Sitting down on the edge of a picnic table, Dolores sighed. "Here's the deal. My parents are getting divorced. My dad's been beating the crap out of my mom for a few years, and now he's started hitting me and Bobby, too." She gave a little, bitter laugh. "You don't know how lucky you are, Meagan. It must be pretty weird having a mom who's lesbo, but at least things at your house aren't all tense and screwed up. I think my mom and dad have always hated each other. I just wish they hadn't waited so long to get divorced."

I had never thought about how good my life with Charlotte and Mom must seem to a lot of my friends. "Oh, Dolores!" I burst out, and threw my arms around her. We hugged each other and cried for a long time.

FIVE MINUTES AFTER I walk back into my apartment in Boston, the phone rings. It's Grandmother Rosser. I drop my heavy duffel bag next to the couch and sit down. Grandmother is excited to tell me that three of her compositions for violin and piano are being performed in public soon. I close my eyes. All I can think of are the green walls of the hospital room, the pain in Charlotte's face as she struggled to sit up, the way her hand sat heavy on my shoulder while I steadied her. Then Grandmother asks briskly, "So, was it warm down in Florida? How is your mother liking it?"

Something inside of me snaps. Once I begin talking, I can't stop: "Well, I think Mom is doing pretty well considering that her partner of eighteen years is dying of cancer. Even if you don't approve of Mom and Charlotte's relationship, if you love Caitie and me, then you have to understand what is going on for us right now. We are losing a *parent*."

It was the first time I've ever known Grandmother to be at a loss for words. A few minutes pass, during which I can hear my own breath hiss into the receiver. Finally, she says, "Darling, you know that you're a dear, sweet girl, and I love you."

We hang up soon after.

But in her own way, Grandmother shows me that she got the message. For the next few weeks, every time she calls, she asks about Charlotte. And five months later, she sends flowers for Charlotte's memorial service, a sheaf of white irises that stands tall among the others.

GETTING CLOSER

Laura Zee

M y dad was outside mowing the lawn when I noticed he was wearing nylons instead of socks with his sneakers.

"Daddy," I asked, "why are you wearing knee-highs?"

"They're just more comfortable, honey," he replied.

I shrugged, and went back to playing with my Matchbox cars.

Soon after that, my parents held a family meeting. "As long as I can remember, since I was a little boy, I've felt different," my dad said. My mom just sat quietly next to my dad. She has always tended not to talk about things she finds upsetting.

My dad said, "There are lots of other people who feel the same way. And there's a name for it—it's called 'cross-dressing.'" That was why he liked wearing women's clothes, he explained, and added that he took female hormones every day, too. He said that female hormones make women's breasts develop.

I peeked at his chest. I had never noticed that my dad had breasts, probably because he wore suits with vests. Dad was a computer specialist, out in the business world. The only thing different about him was that his hair and nails were slightly longer than most of his colleagues, and, as I had just learned, underneath the suit he wore women's underwear.

Learning about my dad's penchant for women's clothing didn't really change anything right away—except that Dad began sleeping in very simple, long, silky nightgowns instead of pajamas. They were usually sleeveless and light blue or pink or beige. My mom wore the same kind. My parents didn't tell me not to talk about my dad to other people. They didn't need to. It was understood that this secret was something that we kept within the family.

After the meeting, when my dad asked me what I was thinking, I told him that he and my mom had always taught us that it was wrong to judge people by how they looked, what religion they were, or what color their skin was. The important thing was that people should be honest and treat each other with respect and kindness. I believed this with all my heart, because as one of the few Jewish kids at our small elementary school, I had learned about intolerance at a very young age. Once a friend told me we could play together at recess, but not after school, because I was Jewish. It never made sense to me, but those were her mother's rules, and I always did what grown-ups said.

So I took the news about my dad at face value, as simply another mysterious, adult fact of life. Besides, my dad still did all the things dads are supposed to do. He encouraged my interest in gymnastics, saved every drawing and craft project I ever made, suffered through Girl Scout father-daughter dinners and Little League games, and beamed with pride the whole time. I was his little girl, and his patience with me was endless. Whereas my mom would get frustrated with trying to comb the tangles out of my long hair and start to tug, my dad would gently and carefully untangle my rat's nest, strand by strand. My mother would threaten to cut it short, but my dad could always be counted on to defend me.

I WENT THROUGH HIGH school with little fear that the family secret would be revealed. My dad did quite a bit of traveling for work during my teen years, and when he was home, he was often tired and grumpy from working too hard. Like the rest of my high school friends, I considered my parents to be tedious, old-fashioned, and too strict. My irritability during this time, combined with my father's grueling work schedule, made our

relationship somewhat strained. I tried to stay away from him
as much as possible. Not until years later did I ask myself if I
might have been confused and ashamed about my dad.

When I was seventeen, I left New York to go to Antioch
College in Ohio. After an initial week of homesickness, I loved
school. I met lots of different kinds of people, from all over the
country and the world, but I never heard about anyone like my
dad. I learned about drag shows and went to several on campus,
but that didn't seem quite the same. For one thing, all the guys
that did drag were gay, and I knew my dad wasn't gay. I knew
one guy who occasionally dressed in women's clothes, but since
he casually joked about it and was also bisexual, I never
equated it with my own situation. I still had the sense that I
was the only one who had ever dealt with anything like this in
her family. Embarrassed, I didn't talk about it with anyone.

During the summer after freshman year, I was living and
working in Boston. My parents were coming to visit, and I had
invited two of my close friends from school, Cliff and Eli, to
join us at my place for dinner. Cliff and Eli were, to say the
least, a *very* demonstrative couple.

"Are you sure your parents will be okay with us being gay?"
Cliff asked.

"Oh, definitely," I assured them. "I mean, my aunt is a lesbian, and if they weren't okay with it before, they have certainly
come to terms with it since."

I didn't mention my dad.

When my parents showed up, I was horrified to see my father wearing a hot pink sweatshirt and jeans. My stomach sank
to my feet, but I acted like everything was normal.

After my parents left, the guys were helping me clean up.
Flicking a plate with a blue dishtowel, Cliff said casually,
"Laura, do you mind if I ask a personal question?"

"Go ahead," I answered, feeling myself start to sweat.

He pointed out the color of my father's sweatshirt, and that
he seemed to have noticeable breasts. "Well, here goes," I
thought. I wasn't quite sure how to start.

"Um, my dad likes . . . my dad is more *comfortable* wearing women's clothes. And he, um, he takes hormones to make him feel better, which is why he has breasts. I mean, it's not usually so obvious, since he wears suits to work. And, um, I've never told anyone this before, and I'd appreciate it if you'd keep it to yourselves."

By the time I was done with my speech, my cheeks were burning and I felt almost dizzy. When Eli opened his mouth to reply, I snapped out, "Let's change the subject," before he could speak. I saw him exchange a perplexed glance with Cliff. We finished drying the dishes in silence and muttered goodnight. As the door closed behind them, I wished that I hadn't said anything.

BACK AT COLLEGE, I immersed myself in women's studies and psychology, writing papers like "Gender Identity Development in Children of Lesbian Mothers," which I convinced myself had nothing whatsoever to do with my family. Since the awkwardness of the summer, I was bound and determined not to think about my father at all. If there was something to think about, then it meant there was a problem; and if there was a problem, that meant that I wasn't really fine with my dad; if I wasn't really fine with my dad, that meant I wasn't being tolerant; if I wasn't tolerant of my dad, while I fought for the rights of women and minorities, I was a hypocrite. And that was even worse than being intolerant.

Truth is, I was ashamed of my dad. I thought it was freaky that he felt the way he did. And as long as I pretended to myself and others that he was "normal," I didn't have to face my guilt about those feelings. So that's where I left it during college. My dad wore a suit to my graduation, but I still squirmed all through the commencement address, casting surreptitious glances to the audience where my dad sat, grinning from ear to ear. I was concerned that others might see something askew, but nobody seemed to notice. Or if they did, they never let on.

DIRECTLY AFTER GRADUATION, I moved to Michigan. After a few years, I decided to go back to school and study for my master's degree in social work, little knowing that I would soon find myself facing up, finally, to the struggle I had buried for so long.

Since I was planning to work with people affected by HIV, I was sure to take the *only* class in my program that focused on interpersonal practice with gay, lesbian, bisexual, and transgender people. Of course, I refused to ask myself if I might have a more personal reason for wanting to take the class. But on the first day of class, when the professor passed out the syllabus, I snatched it up eagerly and, without thinking, flipped it open to the section headed "Transgender Issues." To my chagrin, there were no reading assignments listed, just a brief note "to be assigned."

Without stopping to ask myself why reading about transgender people was so crucially important to my future work with gay men and HIV, I cornered the professor after class and asked why that part of the syllabus was blank. He was a fairly young man, with wire-rimmed glasses that he pushed up his nose with one finger while he answered my questions. "There'll be plenty of readings," he replied calmly. "I am just taking a little time to find out how much the class already knows before I decide what to assign. I've also lined up a number of guest speakers to talk to the class about transgender issues: sex reassignment, drag, cross-dressing. . . ."

My stomach began to roil. The distress on my face must have alerted the professor, because he stopped speaking, looked at me for a moment, then said, "Why don't you come back to my office so we can talk about this more?"

I nodded, clutching my papers, and followed him out of the room. Thus began my relationship with David, my professor and adviser; I began talking with him every week, and one day, I told him my terrible secret.

We were sitting in his office talking about class, when I suddenly felt I *had* to tell him. I started speaking before I could change my mind: "I took this class for lots of reasons, most of which I shared during class introductions. The main reason, the one I didn't share is . . ." My heart was pounding so hard I felt like I couldn't breathe. "My dad is transgender, and I wanted to learn more."

David didn't miss a beat. Probably, he'd had some inkling of the truth beforehand. He leaned forward and replied, "Laura, I really want to encourage you to share your story with the rest of the class." Nervous, but also excited and feeling a sense of newfound liberation, I agreed. My classmates, to my relief, were uniformly supportive, congratulating me on my courage and thanking me for sharing so much of myself.

The next thing I had to do was tell my boyfriend, Jim. I was anxious just thinking about it. I really loved Jim: he would be the first boyfriend I had ever told, and the person whose reaction I cared most about. With graduation looming close, I knew I had to tell him soon, but still I kept putting it off.

Then, one afternoon, Jim and I were at a juice bar. A woman sat down next to us and I immediately noticed that she was a male-to-female transsexual. Jim didn't realize until he heard the bass voice coming from the perfectly lipsticked mouth. His jaw dropped and his eyes widened. As we were leaving, he hissed in my ear, "That woman was a man!"

I realized that there could never be a stronger sign that now was the time to tell Jim about my dad. We ended up sitting in my car for hours, having a long conversation about my father and what it means to be transgendered, while damp leaves from the maple tree overhead blanketed the windshield in deep red. I explained that I still struggled to fully accept my dad but that, nevertheless, I loved him for who he was. As the roofs of downtown businesses began to glow in the sun, I told Jim that my dad helped make me who I was, and that, if Jim loved me, then my dad must have done something right.

I was afraid to look at Jim after I stopped speaking. I stared out the window at the darkening street. Then I felt his hand against my cheek. "Hey," he said softly, "as far as I'm concerned, your dad did everything right." Incredibly relieved, I turned around and buried my face in his chest, feeling his arms close around me. Later that night, I admitted to Jim how worried I still was that his family would disapprove if they knew. He told me that his family had plenty of problems, too. "And even though Papa and Mama may be closed-minded about some things," he added, "they treat everyone they meet with respect. They won't say anything to embarrass you."

Even though we later broke up, Jim remains one of my greatest supports in coming to terms with my feelings about my father. After telling him, I found the courage to tell other people in my life even to speak publicly about the subject. And recently, I finally told my dad how much I struggle with my shame and fear about his gender identity. I had never been that honest with him before, and it was quite shocking and painful for both of us. But after hours of yelling and crying from both sides, we ended up sitting together in the living room, my dad on the couch, me nestled on the floor in front of him. He touched my hair, short now—no longer the rat's nest he used to untangle so gently. "I love you, Dad," I said sadly.

"I love you too, Laura," he answered. "And I'm proud of you." I wished I could tell my dad, who had always been there for me, that I was proud of him, too. I couldn't. I'm not there yet.

But I'm getting closer.

TURNING INWARD

Kris Giesing

When I first met Elly, I thought she was a man. Later, when she found out I liked pencil puzzles, she presented me with two that had obviously been taken from *Playboy*. On my twelfth birthday she gave me four actual issues of *Playboy*. (My mother, despite her previous protestations that "there's nothing wrong with appreciating the beauty of the female form," confiscated them a few months later.) Elly also had these cool hand-held versions of Breakout! and video football, which she let my brother and me play with as much as we wanted.

Her generosity made me uncomfortable: she tried too hard to make us like her. But when Mom asked me whether it would be all right if Elly moved in, such objections seemed unkind. It wasn't until I woke up in the middle of the night with Mom and Elly screaming at each other in our driveway that I knew something was seriously wrong.

My mother and Elly sat Karl and me down in our kitchen not long after that incident. "We need to talk about something important," she said. The news of the divorce had been similarly broken: the four of us in the kitchen, Mom doing all the talking, Dad silent and ashen beside her.

"After a great deal of discussion with Elly, I've come to realize that I'm an alcoholic," Mom told us.

I recalled a six-pack that had sat around in the kitchen for several weeks before Elly moved in with only one can missing. I was confused; for the life of me I could not understand how she expected such a blatant falsehood to fly.

"No, you're not," I said after exchanging a glance with Karl.
My mother then told us that she and Elly were going to attend Alcoholics Anonymous meetings. I looked at Elly with newly opened eyes: of course, *she* was the alcoholic. However I quickly realized that pursuing the issue would be pointless. Karl and I let the matter drop, though I could see in my mother's eyes that she knew *we* knew the truth.

ONE DAY AFTER SCHOOL, as my friend, Brian, and I were playing catch in the backyard with a Wiffle ball, Elly leaned out of the window of the bedroom she shared with Mom and yelled irritably, "Will you please keep it down so I can get some rest?" It was perhaps three-thirty in the afternoon, and we hadn't been making much noise, just calling back and forth, laughing.

"Want to go over to the field at school?" I asked Brian.

"Sure," he said, but after we had walked there, he left, muttering that he had to get home.

Elly was unemployed for several months. Then she joined an outfit called Pyramid Insurance, which sold term life insurance over the phone. Elly would stay at home making calls, pad and pencil in front of her next to the phone book, reading the same lines over and over.

"Good afternoon," she'd say, "I'm calling on behalf of Pyramid Insurance, and we have a special offer. . . ." I never heard the entire speech.

Elly's recruiter from Pyramid Insurance came over one night to present their sales strategy, which mostly involved recruiting other salespeople. By earning a percentage of your recruits' commissions, you would move up in the Pyramid organization. With all that recruiting going on, I sometimes wondered who was actually selling insurance. Afterward, the recruiter regaled us over meatloaf with his theories regarding the Satanists who slaughtered goats, chickens, and the small children from milk cartons in Indiana's remote cornfields. He had stumbled across such a ceremony, he told us, somewhere west of Kokomo, and was now afraid that the cultists would discover his identity and hunt him down. I wondered if any of them invested in life insurance.

Elly was invigorated by the presentation and promptly recruited my mother. Mom's little yellow construction-paper circle went underneath Elly's green one on the wall of our dining room, just above the red one for Elly's recruiter. Thankfully, this was one pretense that my mother did not feel compelled to carry to conclusion: she kept her job at the corn-processing plant.

Of all the deceptions that my mother perpetrated on Elly's behalf, the most damaging involved her sexual orientation. Elly led my mother to believe that, should word escape that she and Elly were lovers as well as roommates, catastrophe and exile would surely follow. Although it is a college town, Middleton is buried deep in the conservative Midwest, so Elly's arguments undoubtedly carried some weight. My mother perhaps thought her career would be jeopardized, but that in itself would not have stopped her naturally honest mouth; she must have thought her silence would somehow protect Elly as well.

Some days after Karl dragged the word *lesbian* out of my mother, Elly explained to me how badly regarded lesbians are by society. She explained that she and my mother might get harassed, perhaps beaten. Murder was unlikely, but not out of the question. The perpetrators might be undereducated Midwestern hicks or alcohol-crazed university frat boys; even the clerk at the corner convenience store might secretly be a member of the Klan, the Grand Wizard of which had recently made local headlines. In short, she implied, it wasn't safe to tell anyone.

But Elly had her own motives for keeping my mother closeted. Unable to discuss even such basic topics as her partnership with Elly, my mother became very socially limited. There is a certain amount of turning inward that comes with a long-term relationship, but the added closet factor made Mom into a virtual recluse. Elly's recruiter coming to dinner is the single incident that I can recall where our house hosted any kind of adult social activity.

My mother was willing to pretend to be straight (and an

alcoholic, and a saleswoman) because she had decided to be Elly's rescuer. Accordingly, Elly assumed the role of victim. At my thirteenth birthday party, Elly pulled my friend Hector aside and had a long talk with him. "I want to apologize for the other day," she told him. "You have to understand that I'm an alcoholic. Even though I'm sober, I'm an alcoholic, because alcoholism is something that doesn't go away when you stop drinking." Hector was silent, quite confused: he'd never met Elly before.

Of course, any openness about their lesbianism would be threatening to Elly, because if Mom made any friends, they would probably question the value of her relationship. Karl and I were there, true, but we were just kids, and our advice was quite handily argued away. "You have to be patient with Elly," Mom would tell Karl and me after one or another outburst, "she's not used to dealing with adolescents."

Although my mother's closeting kept her from the wisdom an adult friend might have provided, she did realize that there were problems. For a while, Mom, Elly, Karl, and I visited a minister-turned-family-therapist named Harold Schmidt, sometimes in pairs (Karl and me, or Mom and Elly; never Mom with anyone else) and sometimes as a group. On our first visit Karl and I had great fun whacking each other with the padded bats that Harold employed as part of his therapeutic process. On our second visit we talked about the divorce and how Karl and I felt about it, whether we were bitter or confused that our parents no longer lived together.

Karl and I had settled our feelings about the divorce before it was even finalized. He screamed and cried while I climbed on top of the unfinished house our parents were building together, where he couldn't follow: I was afraid he might hurt me in his rage. I felt that if Mom no longer had an emotional bond to Dad, their marriage would be pointless; Karl felt betrayed by a supposedly mature adult world.

On our third visit, Harold Schmidt told Karl and me that we were causing the family's problems by our refusal to accept Elly. He claimed that we were hostile because we saw her trying to replace our missing father. Karl and I, having already seen that episode of *Eight is Enough*, refused therapy after that, but Mom and Elly kept seeing him for a number of years.

I saw Harold Schmidt's face once more, years later, on the cover of the *Journal & Courier*: MINISTER DEFROCKED, read the headline. "Therapist Had Sex with Hypnotized Patient." I wonder now whether Elly duped Harold Schmidt with her victim line or whether they recognized something similar in each other that made them cohorts.

In any event, Elly certainly learned the lines. Arguments between Elly and my mother became ritualized, stylized, full of psychobabble lingo. Elly would say matter-of-factly, "Cindy, you always do this to me. Will you stop thinking of just yourself? I have needs, too." Or she would flatly state, "I'm so angry and upset with you right now," which was necessary because usually the only indication of what Elly was feeling was that she would begin to get fidgety and agitated.

In Boston and New York and San Francisco, gay rights activists wrote and marched and rallied and voted because Ryan White had been dismissed from school for having AIDS. In Middleton, my mother avoided reality by working late nights at the office, eating McDonald's Quarter Pounders, gaining weight, confiding in no one.

WE HAD BUILT A house full of rules: Don't talk about this. Don't touch Elly's stuff. Don't upset. Don't disturb. But Elly's were not the only rules; by high school, at which time my nervousness toward her had blossomed into full-scale enmity, I was constructing them, too. I never ate off her plates, read her books, touched her food. I always took her phone messages politely, though I maintained a careful balance of delivery and loss (Elly eventually went out and bought an answering machine). I never made any unnecessary noise around Elly, sleeping or awake. The rules I made for myself were rigid and much more permanent than Elly's demands of the moment. I was trying to beat her at her own game.

I learned to display generosity without warmth, considera-
tion without empathy, courtesy without goodwill. I learned that
it is possible to live with someone for ten years with absolutely
no caring; to remove all the emotional, human components of
communication from every aspect of life and still have the appearance of normalcy. In fact, Elly never seemed to notice or
care that anything was missing.

I remember telling my father once, "My friends and I have
a great relationship because I understand what they're feeling
without them having to say anything." My father gave me an
odd look and said, "Kris, that's not healthy at all."

My father meant that we should be able to express our feelings to each other and not have to rely on guesses, but I was
comparing us with Mom and Elly, who had to spell everything
out for each other in excruciating detail. These spars usually
ended with Mom sighing and saying, "Oh, Elly," in a tone both
patronizing and resigned.

By the time I was in college, Elly had rotated through several
careers and was studying art. One semester she threw a lot of
pottery with a special glazing technique that produced a rain-
bow effect. They were interesting to look at, and I said so, re-
questing one of the pieces as a gift. Elly, of course, was flattered
and agreed. But I had no intention of keeping the little bowl I
picked out. I gave it to a friend to use as an ashtray.

My mother finally broke things off after Elly received her
degree. Maybe the graduation allowed Mom to feel her responsibility toward Elly to be at an end; in any case, I was relieved.

I was even happier when Mom came out of the closet, in
rather spectacular fashion: she agreed to be interviewed for the
local paper. My mother, now a graying "little old lady," was
the last person the townspeople would have pictured as being
a lesbian. She did endure some unfriendliness at first; the neighbors on one side told her not to come to visit their little kids
anymore. But the neighbors on the other side took the news
with aplomb, and she was welcomed by her Unitarian congregation. By now, the mothers of the little kids have thawed a bit.
Really, Mom is about the least threatening person you can

imagine. She has more friends now than I can remember since the divorce.

The last time my mother heard from Elly, she called to say she was selling long-distance service and wanted to know if my mother would like to switch? I picture Elly with another chart in primary colors on the wall, only this time she has her address book in front of her next to the pad and pencil. Elly was prepared to play on Mom's lingering guilt about ending their ten-year relationship to get one commission. I asked my mother whether she was insulted, but she said only that she declined.

My mother is remarried now. I attended her commitment ceremony to a very nice woman named Linda. My father has also remarried, and I even have a half-brother named Brian, who is now a bit over two. They're both happy marriages; neither relationship is better or worse than the other. It is quite a relief, really, not to worry about either of them anymore. I want a T-shirt that says, "I've seen my parents married off, and now I can die happy."

HOME MOVIE

Becky Parker

REWIND

My mom is walking me to school, as he does every day, holding my hand and Carl's leash as we cross the busy streets. We pass the doctor's office on the corner, the gaudy yellow house, and the schoolyard. We pass people waiting for the bus and see other mothers driving by in station wagons filled with kids, preparing to drop them off at the school entrance. I wonder if they notice anything different about my mom since he got his crew cut, and if they whisper about it as we walk by.

FAST FORWARD

"Becky, why does your mom have a beard?" whispers Michelle, playing idly with the zipper to her plaid flannel sleeping bag. My face gets hot and my heart starts to race. My mom has been changing into a man for almost four years now, but this is the first time any of my friends has asked me about him directly. I can hear each second tick by on the wall clock as I search for the right words. *I don't want the world to know that my mom is a man. I don't know if I'm ready to trust anyone with this secret.* But there doesn't seem to be any other way to explain. No half-truths or evasions could begin to describe the years of testosterone therapy and multiple surgeries; the way I struggle to say "Chris" in public so the grocery clerk won't hear me calling the short, bearded man next to me "Mom."

I feel Michelle shifting awkwardly next to me. I am so afraid that she won't want to be my friend anymore, that she'll tell people at school, that everyone will know and will not accept me. Lacking anything more creative to say, I give up—and tell the truth.

"Um, my mom is a man," I mumble, barely able to get the words out.

"Oh." I can't entirely read Michelle's reaction, but she seems curious. "So are your parents homosexual? Or is your mom just a cross-dresser?"

I don't know how to make her understand. My parents got divorced when I started the third grade, before my mom's sex change, which means that my dad was never involved with my mom in a homosexual relationship. My mom isn't a cross-dresser, since being a transsexual and being a transvestite are two different things. And my mom actually dresses pretty much the same way he did when he was a woman, in jeans and flannel shirts. I try, haltingly to explain this to Michelle. She has a million more questions for me, a lot of which I've never even thought about: Is my mom gay, bisexual, or straight? Has he had sex-change surgery? Does he have a penis? How does he go to the bathroom? Does he go out on dates? With men or women? Does he *tell* them?

I stammer through my responses, relying on my limited sex-change vocabulary and a lot of imagination. I feel shell-shocked, part of my brain just wondering if I will still have a social life next week, and if Michelle will understand why this information has to remain just between us.

REWIND

I can think of dozens of men who would have looked more comfortable in a dress than my mom did at my Aunt Allison's wedding. It was two years before my mom began to change, and I still remember how awkwardly she stumbled down the aisle in her puffy satin dress and white low-heeled pumps. I can't accurately distinguish when my mom stopped just looking "masculine," and actually started looking like a man—it was a gradual and natural process. I do remember, though, that I balked at the outward changes that I was afraid would be obvious to my friends and teachers at school. In fifth grade, I threw a fit when my mom said he wanted to get one ear pierced, a tattoo, and a very short haircut—basically a crew cut. I managed to convince my friends that my mom needed to have short hair for work, but the earring and tattoo were harder for me to accept. I thought more people would notice and ask questions. I was surprised to realize, as time went by, that what seemed like glaring physical changes to me were barely perceptible to others. Eventually, I was relieved to see that people were far less observant than I would have thought.

FAST FORWARD

My mom and I are walking through the parking lot on our way to Applebee's. As we pass a group of elderly ladies gossiping on a cement bench, I see their heads swivel to watch us, and I catch the phrase "nice-looking couple." It takes a moment for their meaning to sink in, and when it does, I am mortified that the women think my *mom* is my boyfriend!

This soon becomes a common mistake. As a man, Chris looks much younger than his thirty-seven years: He has a smooth, round face, a few scattered pimples, and a goatee. His shoulders are broad over a trim waist, and he walks with a confidence many people find attractive. When the couple comments start getting too frequent, I playfully threaten to make him wear a big 37 on his shirt unless he starts looking older.

PLAY

I am sitting with my grandparents, my mom's mother and father, on the blue couch in their living room. Grandpa has just said, "I remember when Chris was a little girl . . ." and launched into a story about the time when he was landscaping the backyard, soon after they moved into the house. My mom, who was about eight at the time, was playing nearby and got her feet caught in some loose twine lying on the ground. When my grandpa called to her to come over and get untangled, she just turned around, laughing and ran the other way—and as the twine pulled tight around her ankles, she tripped right over. "She was always a girl with her own mind about things," chuckles Grandma.

It feels strange, listening to Grandpa and Grandma call Chris "daughter" and "girl," but I realize that that's how they knew him for over thirty years. They raised a daughter, only to gain a son they'd never had.

REWIND

We're at the Wendy's drive-through window, my mom digging in her pockets for the bills to pay for my junior bacon cheeseburger and fries. I slurp away at my chocolate Frostee as my mother pays the man at the window, and he hands back her change.

"Here's your change, sir." I look at my mom to see if she will correct him, but she just puts the truck in gear and slides out to the street. After she has turned right, I ask, "Mom, why didn't you tell that man you're a woman?"

She pulls up at a stop sign and turns to look at me. "Because it's no big deal, little monkey," she says, tugging on my ponytail. "No big deal."

PLAY

My mom and I may never have gone to mother-daughter sleepovers or shopped for bras together, but that hasn't stopped him from being a wonderful parent to me. He stopped walking me to school a long time ago, but since we both have busy lives, we continue to spend most of our time together on the run. In my senior year of high school, I would come home from school and drive my mom to do all of his errands after work and before his night class. I would tell him about my day at school, and all the latest news from Michelle (still my best friend) about her new boyfriend; he would dish the dirt on the latest union scandals and about the other guys at work.

It's the same now that I'm coming home from college for breaks: We spend all the time we can together, late at night or in the car traveling from place to place. Sometimes we still visit the Wendy's drive-through for burgers and chocolate Frostees. And when my mom pays for the food, there is no question that the Wendy's employee will hand back his change with a respectful "sir." Every time my mom is called *sir* or *mister* or *him*, I see him quietly beaming, and I realize those small words have never been a mistake—that my mom has finally become the person he wanted to be, and in some ways, had always been.

RITES OF PASSAGE

Daniel Belasco

At Grandpa Ben's funeral, there were the designated mourners and the rest of us who merely grieved.

Sandy, who was officiating at the service, explained that according to custom, only Grandpa's immediate family—meaning Grandma, Aunt Karen, and my mom, Claire—were considered the mourners. "They will wear the torn ribbons that represent their loss," she intoned.

I closed my eyes. I only reopened them once I heard the muffled sobs of my mother. Sandy leaned toward her and, with her right hand, tenderly sliced her ribbon with a razor blade. With her left hand she gently cupped my mother's shoulder. Sniffling, Mom drew a crumpled tissue from her pocket while holding on to her sister for support. Sandy moved from Mom to Aunt Karen to Grandma Lou, carefully slashing each black ribbon pinned to their chests. I stood in the circle next to Mom, watching Sandy comfort each of them and feeling strangely left out. I closed my eyes again and pictured Grandpa Ben. Without thinking, I reached to fondle my own ragged bit of ribbon before remembering I hadn't been chosen to wear one.

SANDY, OR REBBE AS I call her, met my mother in 1985 at Congregation Beth Simchat Torah, the gay and lesbian synagogue in Greenwich Village. After moving up to White Plains, New York, with Mom, my sister, Jude, and me shortly thereafter, Rebbe quickly adopted us as her second congregation. As a Reform rabbi she became the spiritual leader of our family, shaping all our domestic rituals, like Passover seders and Shabbat dinners. Mom and Rebbe created a fully kosher home—something I had never experienced when my mom and dad still lived together—and I began to be exposed to new traditions. And admittedly, I wasn't fond of all of them. That is, I loved celebrating Rosh Hashanah and Hanukkah, but I couldn't bear to stop eating *treyf*, gobbling unkosher yet irresistible bacon cheeseburgers when I went out with friends. As Mom and Rebbe sanctified the Sabbath by going to shul, spending time at home, and foregoing work, I treated Saturday like any other day. And while I grew to anticipate the day when Rebbe would marry me to some unknown beloved under the chuppah, that expectation didn't keep me from eyeing non-Jewish girls.

When Grandpa Ben died, it was decided that Rebbe would officiate at his funeral. I wasn't part of the decision-making process, but I wasn't surprised. Though Grandma is still feisty and Aunt Karen is three years older, my mother is the family ringmaster, with keen leadership skills and a raucous sense of humor honed on the streets of Brooklyn. And once she brought a rabbi into the family, our house naturally became the family's central gathering place. My sister and I were forever adding and removing two massive oak boards from the dining room table in order to accommodate the ever-changing dinner guest list.

After Rebbe moved in, we began having Shabbat dinner every Friday night. The evening was full with ritual, from Grandpa Ben silently filling in crossword puzzles to Grandma Lou devising negative shopping lists ("You have too much lettuce and tuna fish already!") to Rebbe passing out dog-eared photocopies of the Hebrew blessings and their English transliterations. Holding the paper in his slightly trembling hand, Grandpa quietly chanted along with us, using the soft old Yiddish pronunciations that turned every final *t* sound into an *s*. The rest of us sang in a spirited monotone using the harder modern Hebrew pronunciation, nearly drowning out his whispery voice.

Rebbe and Grandpa usually sat near each other at Shabbat, with Grandma on the other side to monitor his food intake. Throughout dinner, Rebbe playfully drew him out with open-ended questions. Early on, he would recount stories about his impoverished childhood in Harlem. But as he grew older and his life smaller, his responses started to trail off into silence. Then, no amount of Rebbe's good-natured cajoling could help.

ONCE WE HAD BEEN ushered into the chapel by the sallow-faced funeral director, Rebbe grabbed my hand and pressed it between hers. Her hands felt cool, though a little damp. "I feel terrible, this is going to be so difficult for your mom," she whispered, her forehead wrinkled with concern as she stared over at my mom.

"No, it will be worse for you," I said. "At least Mom doesn't have to give the eulogy."

I pulled my hand away and watched her take that familiar place behind the podium at the front of the room. She looked so calm, so reassuring back there, paging through her notes, pressing the creases down on her blouse. Like so many times before, I trusted that Rebbe would make sense of this for me. She was given the authority to narrate the life of my grandfather, and somehow, I believed that her speech might make the reality of his death just a little more logical. I felt numb and I needed Rebbe's impassioned, well-chosen words to make his death visceral. I needed her to make me break out of my emotional stupor, just as she had done that previous March.

ON A GRAY AFTERNOON in early spring, Rebbe, Mom, and I went to Auschwitz. The night before our trip was a rough one; I had tossed in my sheets, anxiously watching the digits change on my clock radio. But once I actually saw the barren, snow-covered fields that stretched nearly to the horizon, I couldn't speak. Anything I might say seemed sadly inadequate. Wordlessly, we explored the vast grounds; a smattering of short chimneys were all that remained of the wooden barracks. But when the three of us arrived at a frozen pond where thousands of Jews' ashes had been cast, Rebbe forced Mom and me to talk. Out of her coat pocket, she withdrew three small cards with the Kaddish (a prayer of mourning) printed in Hebrew. When I heard the sound of our three voices reciting the ancient prayer for the dead—*yitgadal v'yitkadash sh'may raba*—tears finally began to creep down my mottled cheeks.

THE FRONT OF THE chapel was a strange tableau. Grandpa's simple pine coffin looked cheap, despite being partially covered by a blue velvet cloth emblazoned with a single white Star of David. The no-frills casket seemed inappropriate for a man who had hand-crafted ornate clocks and toy chests for each of his three grandchildren. And of course, it seemed impossible that such a plain box could hold my grandfather.

Rebbe started recounting Grandpa's history fleeing the Cossacks in 1917, hopping a freighter from Siberia to Seattle with his mother. Quietly she explained how Grandpa Ben's father was not with them on that journey, how Great Grandpa had chosen to leave his family five years earlier to set up their home in America. It was a familiar refrain, one often brought up by Rebbe and my mother to illustrate the importance of commitment to family. Rebbe was speaking slowly, lengthening her vowels in her professional manner, but her voice occasionally quavered. I could see her struggling between being the rabbi and being a mourner, between rhetoric and tears. Many of the stories she told were from decades before I was born, from the Brooklyn days when Mom, Aunt Karen, and their cousins played punchball with Spaldeens. But there were memories I could relate to as well, of how he always greeted his grandchildren with a big bear hug and kiss on the lips, passing on his strength and his tenderness. I was so lost in sepia-toned stories of my mother's youth that I almost forgot to worry about what the other hundred people behind me thought about my lesbian stepmom paying tribute to Grandpa.

Almost. Through the ceremony, I had heard anxious whispers back and forth between Grandpa's friends. *Who is she? I don't have the slightest idea. I never knew Ben had a rabbi for a daughter.*

"The name we call someone indicates what kind of relationship we have with them," Rebbe continued. "To Louise, he was 'My Ben.' To Karen and Claire, he was their 'Pop.' To Daniel, Judith, and Steven, he was 'Grandpa.' And to Mike and me, he was 'Dad.' "

She called him Dad. I looked down, just for a moment, slightly thrown by how deftly she had inserted herself into Grandpa's inner circle, equating herself with my uncle Mike, Aunt Karen's husband. I felt suddenly visible, as if the architecture of my unusual family was on display.

How ironic, I thought, that Rebbe chose to speak about how Grandpa was known by his many names, when I had always struggled to figure out what to call *her*. All through high school, I was unable to tell the complete truth about my pair of mothers, despite the fact that they never gave me the option to shut them out.

Mom and Rebbe always supported my sister and me by coming to our chorus concerts and basketball games, cheering as loudly as every other child-obsessed suburban parent. My task was not deciding whether to let Rebbe come or not—since I didn't have a say in the matter—but how to explain our relationship once she was there. Generally, I squirreled around the issue, calling her my mom's friend. I never managed to call her stepmother, though. I used that word automatically for Dad's wife, Fran, but never for Rebbe.

Eventually the hedging and the semantic games grew tiresome. By my senior year in high school, I decided I was going to go to a peer support meeting at school and say those elusive words: my mother is a lesbian.

I arrived at school that day buzzing as though I were caffeinated. By the end of the day, I could barely sit still. "Before we begin, does anyone want to share something with the group?" Dave, the bearded facilitator, asked. My hand shot up in the air and waved over my head. Twenty classmates turned around to hear my great revelation. I glanced around the room. "I feel that it's important," I fumbled, looking at my shoelaces, "to finally, publicly say that my mother is a lesbian."

As soon as I said it, I realized I had just admitted the obvious. It was as though I had just reported that the world is not actually flat. People politely asked me a few questions, and the discussion quickly turned to other things. I felt relieved, and a little annoyed that I had waited so long.

TWENTY MINUTES INTO THE service, I started to fidget in anticipation of Rebbe's telling of my most important memory of Grandpa Ben. So far, Rebbe had told other family members' touching stories of Grandpa's humor and compassion, and I was sheepish about the morality fable I had given her.

Between dinner and dessert on the night of Rosh Hashanah, circa 1994, Grandpa leaned across the table and quietly said that he had something to ask me. An unusual event, for in my family of loud women and reserved men, Grandpa was the quietest of all. Curious, I stood up and followed Grandpa to the living room, away from the usual din of Mom and Rebbe's uproarious laughter. By the fireplace and mantle that held photos from my Bar Mitzvah, Grandpa leaned towards me, shoulder to shoulder.

"Daniel," he asked, "is your girlfriend Jewish?"

That question again.

Mom had expressed her dissatisfaction with my *shiksa* girlfriend of two years, Gina-Louise, but I interpreted it as another of her innumerable ways of trying to shape my behavior. I challenged her and Rebbe's sometimes intractable standards not because I necessarily disagreed, but because they came to their conclusions so swiftly. So every time my mother challenged me about dating Gina-Louise, I listened to her lecture like an impatient student waiting for the bell. Rolling my eyes, I refused to listen.

Still, she didn't give up. Once, while I was foraging in the kitchen, she informed me that Rebbe does not perform inter-marriages. I was only looking for a cookie, but instead found myself burdened with the fate of the Jewish people. Enough, Mom, I thought with exasperation. Rebbe would happily marry two men or two women as long as they were both Jewish, but she would never officiate at the union of a Jew and gentile, Mom said. The irony did not escape me. Whatever, I snorted.

Gina-Louise was baffled by how my mother valued Jewish tradition over the freedom to love. Your mother is a hypocrite, she spat at me, and you don't have the balls to stand up to her. She was hurt, and I tried to comfort her, but my feelings of bewilderment couldn't match hers of being discriminated against. Even when Gina-Louise stopped calling me when I was at my mother's house, I didn't want to take sides. I still wanted to be with her, but I did not want to sacrifice my relationship with my mother and Rebbe. Besides, I was nineteen, and mar-riage was not so much as a blip on my radar screen. I really wasn't in the mood to consider how the tradition of Judaism hung on who was on the receiving end of my overwrought love letters.

I wasn't sure about my commitment to Judaism, anyway. Twelve long years of after-school Conservative Jewish educa-tion were hardly inspiring: other than memorizing the words to prayers I rarely understood, I learned never to give back a scrap of land to the Arabs, that the Nazis played catch with Jewish babies on bayonets, and to never ever marry out of the faith. We never discussed Judaism and homosexuality, that's for sure. As a religion, Judaism had little meaning for me. If anything, it was a burden to go to Hebrew School, to celebrate holidays that require fasting, to sit in synagogue for an interminable length of time. I wasn't sure why I owed this rather burdensome tradition much of anything.

"Daniel," Grandpa repeated, "is she Jewish?"

"Daniel," he said again. "You should marry a Jewish girl."

I nodded. Sure, Grandpa, I know, I mumbled, and we walked back together to the dining room. I hardly spoke the rest of the evening. When he had his coat and hat on, I slightly hesitated before kissing him goodbye. Grandpa's few words stayed with me, though, as if he had officially codified a rule, which I could freely reject but could not ignore. I was faced with the possibility of losing pride and respect from my family. Grandpa's words breathed life into Mom's rules.

Six months later, Gina-Louise and I said good-bye. I dumped her in a cruel fashion, over the phone while she was on vacation with her mother. I made an ideological decision and tried to force my heart to follow that course. It wasn't just Gina-Louise's shiksa status; I also felt I was too young to be so deeply involved. But it was a little easier to push her away because I had the tacit blessings of my family. I tried to ignore the feeling that I was voluntarily excising a piece of my heart.

In fact, we got back together again twice more before finally calling it quits, and afterwards, I headed off for a semester in Prague. Toward the end of my time there, a friend and I went up to Krakow, Poland, a hotspot of Holocaust tourism. In a fake Jewish café listening to a fake Jewish klezmer band in a depressingly reconstructed once-Jewish neighborhood, Ryan and I had another of our ranging conversations about our identities as Jews. Gesturing with my fork, I said that, the way I saw it, you don't fully actualize yourself as a Jew until you create a Jewish family of your own. This, in most cases, requires a Jewish spouse. I realized I had come to agree with my family. Fifteen years after my mother came out, I finally acknowledged that our family was woven together as much by our Jewish faith as by our stubborn insistence on making family the priority in our lives.

IN THE EULOGY, REBBE sandwiched my memory between a recollection of cousin Steven playing on Grandpa's tummy and Aunt Karen riding with him on a roller coaster. My story was another moving shadow, perhaps not remembered by the others present but seared in my mind.

In a way, I realized later, Grandpa's funeral was my Yom Kippur, the holiest day when your deeds and atonements, written over the past year, are sealed forever in the Book of Life. With Rebbe, my mother's beloved companion, as my medium, I declared to myself and to my family that she would perform my wedding. And that meant Mom's and Grandpa's words, once merely written, were now sealed, too.

THE PERILS OF KNOWING

Alysia Abbott

September 9, 1973: I want to start writing again, more than ever. But who will I write for? Maybe for Alysia so that she might someday know where her parents were at.

F our months after my father died, I finally began cleaning out the closet of our Haight-Ashbury apartment. My father was a notorious pack rat; the apartment was piled with his papers for novels half written and completed, editors' notes, thrift shop fabrics, and costume trinkets. After watching my father suffer from and eventually die of AIDS for much of the last year, the onerous task of clearing out the rented apartment we had called home since I was nine overwhelmed me. Somehow, I imagined that if I just didn't disturb the particular disorder he'd left me, then maybe my life wouldn't really have to change.

Since Dad had no lover or nearby family, the responsibility of caring for him through life and death was mine alone. As much as this might sound like a terrible burden for a twenty-one year old to shoulder, I relished my martyr status and didn't seek out the help that might have been available had I asked for it. With an adolescent's thirst for drama, I stood tall in my tragedy and almost enjoyed how it set me apart from San Francisco's grunge-affected youth.

THE DAY AFTER MY father died I emptied his checking account of its sum total of a thousand dollars and immediately purchased a pair of steel-toe lace-up army boots. Soldier footwear may have been ubiquitous in early 90s San Francisco, but I felt that I uniquely merited a pair. I had emotionally battled my father's disease on the front lines: fixing him dinner, clipping his toenails, wiping up next to the toilet when his aim wavered. And in the stress of watching him suffer night sweats and waste away to skin and bones, I myself grew lean. But though I appeared small, I felt untouchable. In my new boots I walked the streets with an unflinching gaze. Noting the self-conscious posturing of numerous pierced and tattooed peers, I gleaned strength in a quiet conviction that my death-soaked days would render me the victor in any "street-cred" face-off.

In the days following my father's death, I also began to bask in the history I had inherited and how it somehow made me "interesting." I decorated our apartment with relics from Dad's hippie poet past: gold and green wooden-heeled platform shoes, rare David Bowie records, and framed cartoons Dad had drawn to help assuage my childhood fear of monsters. I proudly donned the clothes I found stuffed deep in his dresser: a rose-patterned cowboy shirt with ivory buttons, a sheer silk black jersey with zebra stripes, a well-worn zip-up leather jacket with quilted lining—all far cooler, in my mind, than anything in the stores in the Haight or the Mission district. The weight of my father's leather jacket on my back, and the memory of him wearing it—hands in jean pockets, boyish grin—made me feel protected and close to him.

But as much as I wanted to cloak myself in my father's colorful past, I found an equally strong urge to throw it all off so that I could develop my own life. I recalled bitterly how I had to graduate college a semester early to move back in and take care of him. By the time I'd bought my one-way airline ticket back to San Francisco, I had sowed the seeds of an adult life in New York. I'd found my first apartment outside the dorms, a weekend restaurant job for pocket change, and an internship at a major entertainment company. But in California, I was again the daughter. Upon realizing that I'd sacrificed my budding life to live indefinitely with my sick father, his many pill vials and nurse visits, I had thrown myself onto his bed in a tearful rage.

AFTER MY FATHER'S DEATH, I decided to move back to New York, and to my former independence. But first I had to face the daunting task of sorting through my father's twelve-year accumulation of ephemera. I divided items into loose categories: "throw away," "keep," "sell," "don't know." Progress was slow. Rarely could I make my way through any drawer or box without finding a memento that would engulf me in an hour-long rumination. It was somber and lonely work. Buried in boxes, bags and packing tape I played my stereo loudly for company. In the immediate weeks after my father died I had en-joyed blasting particularly serious, portentous classical works like *Carmina Burana* and Mozart's *Requiem*. Now, anticipating an unburdened life in New York, I preferred classic seventies soul. I was listening to *The Golden Age of Black Music: 1970–1974* the afternoon I tapped the mother lode in the dining room closet.

Four feet deep in old papers, records, and odds and ends, our dining room closet had long been a joke among my closest friends. I had just cleared out a stringless tennis racket, the man-uscript version of my father's last book, and disintegrating clip-pings about orange juice promoter and antigay protester Anita Bryant when I stumbled upon a cache of notebooks. I had found my father's journals, which together traced Dad's life from high school to college to our life together in San Francisco, ending with his last journal written six months before his death, con-taining barely legible scribbles as AIDS-related CMV retinitus began to strip away his vision.

I had always known my dad kept journals. As a young girl, I excitedly waited until he left the apartment to sneak into the milk-crate bookshelves and pull out his two hard black journals looking for descriptions of myself as a toddler—how I inexpli-cably used to call my father "Little Deble" or the time I was unhappy with my spoon. But I never had interest in his quotid-ian thoughts, and after finding a satisfactorily cute reference to me, I would put the books away. As a teenager I had no desire to read my father's journals; I was trying to keep as far away from his "weird" life as possible. But in the wake of his death, the journals in my hands, many of which I'd never seen before and predated my memory, were precious archaeological treasures, passkeys to a lost civilization. I immediately dug in.

Noting the date in the margin of each entry, I homed in on four small spiral notebooks dating from the early seventies. I was born in 1970; my mother, Barbara, died in a freak car accident in 1973. This was the brief period when my dad, mom, and I formed a family in Atlanta.

Because I couldn't remember my mother, I had spent my life getting to know her as the beloved daughter and sister of other people. My grandfather used to proudly show me her report cards and the effusive congratulatory letter her Latin teacher sent the year she graduated as valedictorian. Uncle David recalled how she played first chair clarinet and read *Little Lulu* and *Uncle Scrooge*.

I had always relied on these old photos and family anecdotes to piece together an image of my mother. Now, crouched on the bare wooden floor of our dining room, in ink-smeared yellow-edged pages, she lived again.

> August 28, 1973: Awakened by phone. I'm told, after much hemming and hawing, that Barbara has expired. I start shaking. What to do? What to do? Call Barbara's parents. I ask for her father, say I have bad news, "There's been an accident; Barbara has expired."
> "What are you saying?" her mother shrieks.
> "Barbara is dead."
> "Oh God, no," her mother says, and the phone clicks.

Reading my father's description of the phone call notifying him of my mother's sudden death, I relived her death as if for the first time. But as painful as it was to read, I didn't want to put the pages down. I hungered for this connection and only stopped reading when welling tears made it impossible to focus my eyes.

The grief I felt for my mom manifested in different parts of my body than what I'd felt for my father. Having grieved my dad for the duration of his sickness, as well as after his death, I'd grown accustomed to crying for him in various positions and locations. Now suddenly grieving my mother, I sat immobile, each of my sobs erupting from the lowest reaches of my insides. I howled and hyperventilated. I carried on like this until I was too tired to continue, and as I reawoke to my surroundings, I discovered my CD had long finished playing and wondered if the neighbors had heard me.

I read these three early-seventies journals a couple more times before the move—each reading induced the same intense and exhausting emotional response, which I found myself curiously craving. I then packed and mailed the notebooks along with other dad sentimentalia—a porcelain pair of Scottie dogs I gave him for Father's Day when I was seven, his Queer Nation and "Boys with Arms Akimbo" T-shirts, my primary school stories and drawings he'd saved—and boarded a train to the East Coast.

I spent one month traveling to New York, stopping along the way to visit relatives and friends. In my sleeper car, I typed daily observations into a laptop and felt remarkably free. When passengers I'd meet over dinner inquired about my reasons for traveling I'd give them a simple story. "I'm an NYU student traveling round-trip from San Francisco to New York" was sufficient for most of them. The real circumstances of my trip were too complicated and personal to explain. Whenever I could, I walked the length of the train to the window of the last car. Listening to the loud rattling metal, I watched with a strange relief as the track spilled out from beneath my view and gulped down the growing distance between myself and where I came from.

AS I JUMP-STARTED MY New York life I regretted that I couldn't list "cared for dying father" as "experience" in my résumé. Outside of my father's world, cut off from his piles of papers, the cafés he frequented, his friends and community, there was no place to fit my memories of him. When I missed him I would pull out one or two of his journals and immerse myself in their melancholy dust. For hours, I would sift through reams of pages in search of the capital A, for Alysia, or my childhood nickname A-R. In Dad's descriptions of our life together I found my way back into our bond—the family past only we shared.

> January 18, 1975: Had a lot of fun with A-R in the park. We played Hide and Seek. When she couldn't find me she'd say "Where are you, Daddy?" and I'd say, "Here I am," and then usually she could follow the sound.

Three years after I moved back to New York, my grandparents in Lincoln, Nebraska, mailed me a box of Dad's things because they were "downsizing" their home. The items they had kept, all remembrances of my father's youth, were frozen in time. They sent bronzed baby booties, an army green band stitched over with Boy Scout merit badges, photographs of "little Stevie" in communion whites, school programs and posters he had illustrated—material evidence of the life he lived before my birth. Oddly, the pile of my grandparents' keepsakes made me realize for the first time, somewhat sheepishly, that other people missed him just as much as I did.

Following this trail of breadcrumbs, I added my grandparents' memories to my own and in doing so awakened a desire to piece together my father's biography. I hoped that in learning as much as possible about the man whom I had only known as Dad, and creating something that could be shared, I could maybe bring a part of him back to life. With the help of a web designer friend, I used the Internet to build a detailed chronology tracing my father's life.

I aimed to launch my website, www.steveabbott.com, on Father's Day, 1999. Over the next six months I organized and sifted what my grandparents and I had saved, helped digitize photos and drawings, and typed in letters, journals, poems, reviews, and excerpts from the books my father had written himself. The work was rigorous but deeply satisfying. Finally I could direct my lingering grief toward something tangible, while at the same time lifting from my shoulders the solitary burden of his memory.

Of all of the materials I worked with, my father's journals were the thorniest writings to delve back into. Though some of his old letters painfully reminded me how much I missed him, none of them threatened my identity or my image of my father. A journal might not be such safe reading.

Still, convinced that nothing could be worse than watching my father die, I dove into his journals with a false sense of invincibility. I planned to sift the pages for facts, immune to the emotional fallout of Dad's uncensored musings, and compose his story like a reporter or detective. Since we had been so close, I assured myself there would be nothing I could find that I couldn't handle. And yes, I succeeded at being remarkably detached at times—scrutinizing his life unjudgmentally as his biographer, not as his daughter.

> June 6, 1973: Going to Frisco it was easy to be born again. How to continue doing so when living in the midst of hassles so familiar is the challenge. Going to Stone Mountain with Barb and A-R was fun at first, then a tired duty, which wilted into an unbearable feeling of being trapped, oppressed and sucked dry. Why is this? Is it insanity that I cannot be satisfied with Barbara? At night I go out to the bar where the dim lit haze of smoke is a backdrop for smiles, drinking, sweaty dancing, and seeking sex with some attractive man stranger who may perhaps lift me out of this world.
>
> Had good conversation with Barbara after writing the above. I discussed that I wanted to live alone and talked about my other relationships. Often when we discuss things Barbara cries, gets upset or defensive. This time more than any other I can recall, Barb seemed to accept me as a free agent and not make any demands. Now I'm not sure I want to move out.

As a child I believed that my parents had known a fairy-tale love that was shattered only by my mother's fatal car crash. I imagined their meeting like a maiden and a prince: my hand-somely hetero Dad asking my beautiful brown-eyed mother to go steady, marry him, then give birth to his glorious baby. I blamed her car crash alone for the difficulties of my childhood: the bullies that called me "weird" and forced me to eat orange peels, the embarrassment I felt that I had no mother to braid my hair or make Rice Krispies Treats for class parties. If she hadn't died, I then reasoned, my father wouldn't have "turned" gay, and I would have fit in at school.

Eventually, in my teens, I came to realize this narrative I dreamed up was a myth. My father never told me outright about their conflicts and respective infidelities, of course, per-haps in order to protect the beatific image I held of my mother. But he did hint that their marriage could have ended in divorce. And for a brief period in high school, I even perversely consid-ered myself lucky to have been spared the parental split that so many of my friends suffered through.

By the time my father died, I knew my parents' relationship wasn't a great romance, and I had even learned that they'd each taken lovers. Nonetheless, I was disappointed to find that none of Dad's journals mentioned my parents *ever* being in love. Worse, Barb appears not as the beaming-valedictorian-clarinet-playing mother of my imagination but as a needy wife who gave good boyfriend advice. Rather than containing thoughtful de-scriptions of their relationship, my father's journals are instead filled with pages of musings, unsent letters, and poems anguish-ing over his lover John's cool indifference.

June 26, 1973: Come home depressed about John. Should I tear up book of poems, put the pieces in an envelope and mail it to him? Barb says ignoring someone is better than a dramatic ges-ture but in John's case I don't know; he is so passive. I want to see him but I don't want to call him. Again I feel alone. Been thinking about moving out and living alone again but I can never make up my mind. Don't want to spend too much money or get more isolated than I want. Mainly I want to stay close to A-R.

Though in these journals Dad's descriptions frequently return to his deep love for me, I couldn't help but feel angry and betrayed by how he obviously neglected my mother. I knew he loved her but I wanted him to give her the passion that he reserved for men. Reading my father's journals I started to feel like an accomplice to his betrayal because I could only report his point of view, which, of course, I couldn't change. I considered my grandmother and remembered her curiously cold behavior toward my father. And one night, I telephoned her to sympathize with the pain she must have felt as my mother's mother.

May 16, 1974: Feel tired from carrying A-R around all day. Read her some stories, the same three as last night: "Tom Thumb," "The House that Jack Built," "10 Apples on Top." Put her to bed. She cries because I won't let her wash her baby. I hold her a while and she goes to bed happy.

Throughout my childhood, I held tightly to my belief in Dad's unwavering love for me. I regularly tested this conviction through tantrums and demands for his attention. I remember once stubbornly commanding him to sit on a snail during a game of Simon Says and the crunch sound after he grudgingly obliged me. My faith in this devotion kept a rein on the anger I may have otherwise felt about his being poor, gay, and not my mother. I forgave him these transgressions because in his arms I felt safe.

But upon close study of his journals, I was disturbed to read pages and pages without finding any capital As or A-Rs. As with my mother, my place in his journals were often co-opted by Dad's love interest of the moment and later by his work.

March 13, 1974: Without Chris, I feel very lonely again but trapped and unable to find relationships while I have the responsibility of A-R. A-R continues to be extremely demanding, stubborn and clinging. Went to Mary's for dinner. Felt exhausted and beaten down. A-R spilled my drink and I got angry—jumped around and yelled. A-R looked at me wide-eyed. I told her I still love her. She refused to eat any dinner and clung to me, making it hard to talk.

Need to call the Sullivans to see if they can take her for awhile.

It sounded familiar. I remembered fearing my dad's sudden bursts of anger, which led to my terrified nightmares that he would abandon me and that I would die alone in the snow like the Little Matchgirl. But reading these harried entries I felt angry all over again. I felt angry at my Dad for not being sensitive to my natural loneliness and fear after losing my mother. I felt angry that he didn't provide me a stable home and regularly passed me off to neighbors so he could go cruise the bars.

But after my tenure as his caretaker, I could also understand his frustration. Once, agitated by one of Dad's coughing fits while I was studying for the GREs, I had yelled "Shut up!" and immediately wanted to swallow my words. I imagined myself as a recently widowed parent overwhelmed by caring for a small child, much as I had felt burdened by caring for my father through his sickness. I knew I could have reacted just as he did.

October 28, 1986: Why is everyone I'm attracted to either too young or vapid and flaky? I can't seem to feel anything for anyone normal, sensible, or less than impossibly beautiful. And how could I get anyone past Alysia? I met Paul at the Café Flore. Too noisy so we came back to my place. Then Alysia interrupted not once, but twice—blowing the scene for me. She insisted I go look at this dress with her, Paul said "I'm going anyway" and I couldn't help wondering if that was why.

I remembered my early efforts to sabotage my father's romances. With few exceptions, Dad attracted lost-sheep types who not only distracted his attention from me but who might have easily stolen our hairdryer. And since none of Dad's boyfriends lasted, I treated anyone who entered our lives as an intruder or simply ignored them. My rude behavior prevented anyone from getting close, but I'd never really considered my father's disappointment or frustration.

Now, I felt momentarily guilty, wondering if my childish self-absorption had prevented my father from having a loving relationship. But reading through my father's journals and stumbling upon descriptions of myriad brief sexual encounters made me feel hostile and suspicious all over again. Which of these men, I wondered, gave my dad HIV?

MONTHS AFTER LAUNCHING MY website, while casually reading one of my dad's journals, I discovered that he tested positive for HIV in 1986. I was in shock. My dad had gotten his test results while I was fifteen and still living at home, more than two years before he finally revealed his status to me. I couldn't fathom how Dad could keep this secret from me. I felt betrayed by my memory and also by my father. I had thought that we trusted each other with everything. A hollowness filled my chest. How could I claim to have authority over my experience, or claim, as I did on the website, that my father and I were "so close" if I was ignorant of the date he contracted HIV? I began questioning all of my research and feeling my website was fraudulent. Briefly, I considered shutting it down.

But then I considered the alternative. Learning that my father carried a fatal virus would have devastated me as a teenager. I was grateful that, by withholding this information, Dad spared me these years. He came to terms with HIV alone, sacrificing his own need for sympathy and comfort to allow me a seminormal adolescence.

Besides, I couldn't help recalling our last moment together, as I sat with him at his deathbed, tracing the blue veins in his hand with my finger. Nothing could take away that final act of trust we shared.

March 16, 1986: Alysia went to see my therapist Francis with me. She seemed very reluctant and a bit hostile. But we both expressed our feelings about things. Francis said he was impressed how much we love each other and how well we were doing against all the odds: I'm gay, we don't have much money and live in a small apartment. I emphasized responsibility matters. Alysia said that she doesn't like me to be just screwing around. I talked about how I felt when she interfered with my love life. We agreed to make cookies and watch Creature Features on TV.

I still get scared of forgetting my father when he was alive— particularly fifteen to twenty years hence, when the number of years I will have lived without him will surpass the number I lived with him. All my life, I clasped photographs in order to know my mother while enjoying the luxury of holding onto my dad's arms and shoulders. I would hate, in my fading memory, for Dad's photographs to become similarly overvalued.

In our fondest memories, we can easily idealize the dead. But, thanks to my father's journals, my feelings toward my dad shift all the time, as in any day-to-day relationship. I get angry, annoyed, disappointed. Sometimes I feel guilty, other times, forgiving. My father speaks to me from the dead, and I talk back.

CONTRIBUTORS

Alysia Abbott was raised in San Francisco. She graduated from New York University in 1992 with a degree in French civilization and political science. On Father's Day, 1999, she launched the acclaimed web site www.steveabbott.com in memory of her late father. She is currently employed at the New York Public Library and is working on publishing a memoir and a Steve Abbott reader.

Daniel Belasco is a freelance writer who has written for *Ms.*, the *Forward*, and a variety of other publications. A native of Westchester, New York, he graduated from Amherst College.

Laurie Cicotello recently completed her M.A.T. in secondary language arts at Hastings College. Laurie is the national contact person for the support group TAKOTS (Teenage Kids Of T's). She served on the Board of Directors for Colorado's Speakers' Project to End Discrimination from 1995–1998.

Kelley Conway is a lesbian-feminist performance poet, playwright, and novelist. She recently finished a first novel, and is now an M.F.A. candidate in theater at Brandeis University. She lives in Massachusetts with her partner of 13 years. A version of her essay appeared in *Girlfriends* magazine.

Maria De La O is the managing editor at *Industry Standard* magazine. She has also written for the *San Francisco Examiner, New York Daily News, Advocate,* and *Curve,* among other publications. She lives in San Francisco.

Jennifer DiMarco is the author of more than a dozen books, most recently *Immortality.* She is owner of the independent press Pride & Imprints. The full version of her essay appears in the anthology *Generation Q* (Alyson Publications).

Kris Giesing lives in Pacifica, California, where he pursues his interests in computers, music, and writing. This is his first publication.

Sophia Gould is the pseudonym of a writer living in Pennsylvania. She holds an M.F.A. in fiction and currently teaches creative writing at a small liberal arts college. This is her second book publication.

Morgan Green is a teenager living in Mill Valley, California. She enjoys acting, writing poetry, and making web pages. This is her first publication.

Christopher Healy is a researcher at *Teen People* magazine. Until recently, he worked as a professional actor, performing in several national and international tours. He has previously written reviews for www.kozmo.com. He graduated with honors from Long Island University in 1995. This is his first published essay.

Stefan Lynch is a Canadian living in San Francisco who is a founding member of COLAGE (Children of Lesbians and Gays Everywhere). He is a vegan chef who delivers meals by bicycle and regularly writes about the politics of food.

Becky Parker is the pseudonym of a freshman at a college in the northeast. This is her first publication.

Julie Diana Rawley resides in Seattle. She is currently at work on a novel, *Victory Garden.*

Meagan Rosser is a mental health counselor and massage therapist living in Somerville, Massachusetts. This is her first published essay.

Peter Snow is the pseudonym of a writer based in New York. This is his first published essay.

Rivka Solomon is the pseudonym of a writer who is currently editing *That Takes Ovaries: Bold Females and Their Brazen Acts*, a collection of true stories by gutsy girls and women to be published by Crown Press. Her essay in this collection is an excerpt from the memoir she is writing about growing up female in America in the 1960s and 1970s.

Meema Spadola is a producer, director, and writer. She recently produced and directed *Our House: a very real documentary about kids of gay and lesbian parents* that premiered on PBS in 2000 and was funded by ITVS (Independent Television Service) and the Soros Documentary Fund of the Open Society Institute. With Thom Powers, she previously produced *Private Dicks: Men Exposed* for HBO and the award-winning *Breasts: A Documentary*. Her book *Breasts: Our Most Public Private Part* (Wildcat Canyon Press) was published last year.

Tristan Taormino is the author of *The Ultimate Guide to Anal Sex for Women* and director, producer and star of the video based on her book. She is the editor of *On Our Backs* magazine and series editor of the Lambda Literary Award–nominated collection *Best Lesbian Erotica*. She is a regular columnist for the *Village Voice* and the sex advice columnist for *Taboo* magazine. She also produces her own web site, www.puckerup.com.

Ian Wheeler-Nicholson is a writer based in New York. He is working on his first novel. A version of this essay previously appeared in the *San Francisco Bay Guardian*.

Jeffrey Wright is the pseudonym of a nineteen-year-old who is studying to become a pilot.

Laura Zee is the pseudonym of a writer living in Ann Arbor, Michigan. This is her first published essay.

ABOUT THE EDITORS

Noelle Howey is a freelance writer and a previous contributing writer at *Seventeen*. She has written for *Ms.*, *Time Out New York*, *Glamour*, *Jane*, *Mademoiselle*, *Mother Jones*, *Talk*, *Brooklyn Bridge*, *Parents*, *Teen People*, *YM*, and many other publications. She is currently working on a family memoir for Picador USA. A native of Cleveland, Ohio, Noelle graduated from Oberlin College in 1994.

Ellen Samuels is an award-winning poet and essayist whose writing has appeared in *The Lesbian Review of Books*, *The American Voice*, *Kalliope*, and many other journals and anthologies. She earned a B.A. in English at Oberlin College and an M.F.A in creative writing at Cornell University, and is now working on a memoir. She is currently a Ph.D. candidate in English at the University of California, Berkeley.

RESOURCES

BOOKS

Allen, Mariette Pathy. *Transformations: Crossdressers and Those Who Love Them.* New York: Dutton, 1989.

Benkov, Laura. *Reinventing the Family: Lesbian and Gay Parents.* New York: Crown, 1994.

Boenke, Mary. *Trans Forming Families: Real Stories About Transgendered Loved Ones.* Imperial Beach, CA: Walter Trook Publishing, 1999.

Buxton, Amity Pierce. *The Other Side of the Closet: The Coming-Out Crisis for Straight Spouses and Families.* New York: J. Wiley, 1994.

Drucker, Jane. *Families of Value: Gay and Lesbian Parents and Their Children Speak Out.* New York: Insight Books, 1998.

Kacscr, Gigi. *Love Makes a Family.* Edited by Peggy Gillespie. Boston: University of Massachusetts Press, 1999.

Pollack, Jill S., *Lesbian and Gay Families in America: Redefining Parenting in America.* New York: Franklin Watts, 1995.

Rafkin, Louise. *Different Mothers: Sons and Daughters of Lesbians Talk About Their Lives.* Pittsburgh: Cleis Press, 1990.

Rudd, Peggy J. *Cross Dressers: And Those Who Share Their Lives.* Katy, TX: Pm Pub, 1995.

Saffron, Lisa. *What About the Children? Sons and Daughters of Lesbian and Gay Parents Talk About Their Lives.* London: Cassell Academic, 1997.

Savage, Dan. *The Kid: What Happened After My Boyfriend and I Decided to Go Get Pregnant.* New York: Dutton, 1999.

Tasker, Fiona L., and Susan Golumbok. *Growing Up in a Lesbian Family: Effects on Child Development.* New York: Guilford Press, 1997.

MAGAZINES

Alternative Family Magazine
P.O. Box 5650
Riverforest, IL 60405-5650
(800) 256-8519
www.altfammag.com

Gay Parent Magazine
P.O. Box 750852
Forest Hills, NY 11375-0852
(718) 793-6641
www.gayparentmag.com

In the Family: The Magazine for Lesbians, Gays, Bisexuals and Their Relations
P.O. Box 5387
Takoma Park, MD 20913
(301) 270-4771
www.inthefamily.com

Transgender Tapestry
P.O. Box 540229
Waltham, MA 02454-0229
(781) 894-8340
www.ifge.org/tgmag/tgmagtop.htm

ORGANIZATIONS

All Our Families Coalition
P.O. Box 16510
San Francisco, CA 94116
(415) 681-1960
www.allourfamilies.org

Alternative Family Project
(415) 436-9000
www.baylinks.com/~afp

COLAGE (Children of Lesbians and Gays Everywhere)
3543 18th Street #17
San Francisco, CA 94110
(415) 861-KIDS
www.colage.org

Family Pride Coalition
P.O. Box 34337
San Diego, CA 92163
(619) 296-0199
www.familypride.org

International Federation for Gender Education
P.O. Box 229
Waltham, MA 02154-0229
(617) 894-8340
www.ifge.org

Lambda Legal Defense and Education Fund
120 Wall Street
Ste. #1500
New York, NY 10005-3004
(212) 809-8585
www.lambdalegal.org

National Gay and Lesbian Task Force
Family Issues Project
1517 U Street NW
Washington D.C. 20009
(202) 332-6483
www.ngltf.org

PFLAG (Parents, Families and Friends of Lesbians and Gays)
1101 14th Street NW
Ste. #1030
Washington D.C. 20005
(202) 638-4200
www.pflag.org

We Are Family
P.O. Box 30734
Charleston, SC 29417
(803) 937-0000
www.waf.org

INTERNET RESOURCES

Family Q
www.studio8prod.com/familyq/

Families Like Mine
www.familieslikemine.com